Why ChatGPT is a Game-Changer

Denis Boulanger Ph.D.

Published by Denis Boulanger, 2023.

WHY CHATGPT IS A GAME-CHANGER

First edition. May 14, 2023.

Copyright © 2023 Denis Boulanger Ph.D..

ISBN: 979-8223539926

Written by Denis Boulanger Ph.D..

Table of Contents

Introduction

Throughout my childhood, much to my mother's dismay, I accumulated a large quantity of toy parts in my bedroom closet I would collect and have fun disassembling when these toys no longer worked. Small electric motors, wheels, gears, marbles, accessories of all kinds, besides Meccano and Lego parts, made up the basis of my games and little "inventions."

My favorite game was building Rube Goldberg machines, or what I called at the time action-reaction machines. These machines allow you to do simple things, like opening a box, by performing a series of complex operations. To do this, you must assemble a series of elements (e.g., rocker, slide) to create a domino effect, resulting in the ending task being accomplished. For example, by throwing a simple marble on a slide, the marble hits a falling block at the end of its course, which activates a switch, which activates a motor, which winds a rope linked to the lid of a box that opens (phew!) The more complex the string, the more interesting the game was. I could spend hours creating these infernal machines that covered a good part of my room.

As a teenager, I loved to imagine and try to make machines of all kinds: a glider, a hydrofoil, a balloon, parachutes with little green soldiers. I read the biographies of great inventors and scientists, such as Edison, the inventor of the electric light bulb, and Marie Curie, made famous for her research on radioactivity. Their lives fascinated me, and they were my heroes. Very early on, I discovered the joys of creation, invention, and discovery. In short, it predestined me to become an inventor one day. Yes, I am a geek and I know it.

I have been working in applied research and innovation for almost thirty years. I am a specialist in computer vision, one of the main axes of what is now called artificial intelligence or AI. This branch of AI comprises designing intelligent systems that allow computers to see and recognize the surrounding things, much like the human eye does.

My passion for computers has led me to develop dozens of different applications, ranging from machines for sorting lumber to one's sorting plastic containers. The scientific games of my childhood helped me develop this ability to create and find solutions to complex problems. In my professional life, they often assigned me projects that were difficult because I often brought a different perspective. My favorite motto describing my way of thinking is "think outside the box."

When I first started writing this book, I wanted to share my experience as an innovator with you, but I soon realized that the subject had been covered many times by various authors much better known than I am. Indeed, by doing some research, I swiftly realized that there are many dozens of books on the subject. Most of them offer "infallible" tips and methods to help people innovate and are mostly addressed to all the aspiring Steve Jobs. But a particular event occurred that changed the course of my thoughts.

WHY CHATGPT IS A GAME-CHANGER

In November 2022, the company Open AI launched a new application called ChatGPT, a natural language processing technology based on GPT-3 (Generative Pre-training Transformer) technology. This revolutionary technology is an approach to natural language processing and has led to the development of many applications in various fields, including high-quality text generation, machine translation, question answering, and many others.

The dialogue model, according to Open AI, allows ChatGPT to respond to many written queries, including theoretical essays, mathematical solutions, and stories. It can answer follow-up questions and, depending on the context, admit that it made a mistake.

I was very surprised (I would even say "flabbergasted") by performing this chatbot (and God knows I've seen some AI-sauce applications). You can ask it many questions in almost any field. Besides using its huge knowledge database, ChatGPT understands and uses the context of the conversation to generate answers related to it.

Before what I could call "the ChatGPT event," I imagined that if we could create a form of artificial intelligence that would analyze the data available on the Web, structure it and set up links and conceptual relationships between them, and that we would use this knowledge to encourage our own creative process, we would reach a higher level of intelligence that would unite both human and computer intelligence. This is exactly what ChatGPT and similar technologies bring.

Like I said, my intention was to express my views on innovation, a subject that has been a significant part of my life since childhood. However, my attention was captured by the fascinating path of ChatGPT, prompting me to wonder: can computers really create or innovate by itself and generate works of art or masterpieces?

Isn't creation the result of a process of intelligence where we mix different ideas to create works or a new machine? Therefore, with all the knowledge we can find on the Web today, why are computers still unable to invent things? What is the difference between humans and machines on this point?

This simple question forced me to think about what intelligence is and how it can create new or brilliant things. This reflection allowed me to ask fundamental questions: What is creation? Are only humans capable of creating? What are the conditions for a person or any other natural or artificial entity (such as computers) to create? Is it possible to imagine other forms of intelligence than ours?

It is only in the last 50 years that we have begun to understand how our brain works, and there is still a long way to go. Although we can describe the creative process, we know little about the underlying physiological and biological mechanisms. However, even if we don't know how it works, we can still describe what the essential conditions are for us to create.

Obviously, when I speak of creation here, I am not only talking about artistic creation such as composing music or painting. No, I am talking about creation in the broadest sense, the creation of new ideas, of inventions, and even scientific discovery, which underlies the creative process. Engineers, researchers, scientists, and architects create many things, sometimes useful and sometimes as beautiful as the works of artists of the Renaissance (at least, from my point of view!), even though the two types of creation do not discuss the same feelings.

This book is for all technophiles who are fascinated by the advances of artificial intelligence to wonder in which direction this technology is heading. Many people believe that artificial intelligence will soon replace and even surpass human intelligence. I will try to show you we are still very far from reproducing all the complexity of our brain. However, we must still ask ourselves the essential questions about the place of this technology in our society. Should we view AI as a threat or an ally that will elevate our intelligence to new heights?

Book Structure

THROUGHOUT HISTORY, many philosophers have considered the definition of intelligence. People thought (and still think to some extent) that intelligence includes a material part, the body, and an intangible part, such as the human soul, for a long time. Despite not having proven that the soul does not exist, we increasingly believe we can explain our thoughts and the functioning of our intelligence by physicochemical processes due to the advancement of knowledge in the functioning of our brain. In either case—the soul versus cybernetics—we must take a leap of faith.

Beyond our understanding of what intelligence is, we can also ask why human intelligence is so different from that of other animals. What were the conditions necessary for the emergence of intelligence and how did it give us the power to create things that no other living being has done before? This will allow us to put into perspective the complexity of our brain compared to other intelligence, be they animal or electronic.

For the past few decades, we have been trying to reproduce some of our brain's functions thanks to the invention of computers. What is now called artificial intelligence is, in fact, a series of algorithmic methods that mimic the functions of our brain. Like us, they can learn how to recognize shapes or details in images by observing them, without being told, how to do so.

When I was a Ph.D. candidate in the 1990s, AI was very popular in academia. But it wasn't until the early 2010s that the AI craze really took off. New deep learning algorithms and, let's face it, a lot of risk capital propelled this technology to the top of the technology charts. Today, most tech gadgets use AI. Many of my clients want AI in their product (even if not always possible). After an overview of the brief history of this technology (I like to tell stories), I will show you how today's researchers have created some amazing applications. I will discuss the latest advances in artificial intelligence and show their power, but also their limitations.

Once the concepts of natural and artificial intelligence are well understood, we must try to define how our ideas can emerge from this organic or silicon-based material. Are strokes of genius the result of a divine inspiration or of a natural process? What are the necessary and sufficient conditions for an intelligent being to create or innovate? Can only humans create?

After trying to answer some of these existential questions, I will propose a five-level classification of intelligent systems according to their creative power. I will show how this definition allows us to compare the diversity of animal and human intelligence by comparing their ability to process and organize knowledge to create new objects or works of art. It will also allow us to better position artificial intelligence with human intelligence and demonstrate that we are still far from being able to reproduce our brains in machine code.

This new definition of intelligence in terms of its ability to create, lays the foundation for a new form of intelligence: a mixed intelligence where natural systems are combined with machines, which will allow us to benefit from the phenomenal amounts of data available on the web to help us create things that were previously unimaginable.

We know today that speech and writing have allowed us to perpetuate our ideas from generation to generation and to produce new ideas or concepts based on the ideas of our forefathers. In the same way, the universal knowledge of the web, available at our fingertips, can take us to a new level of creation. This is what I call "mixed intelligence."

To do this; however, we must be able to understand how we structure our knowledge and how similar methods can structure the knowledge contained on millions of computers around the world. Mixed intelligence could increase our own collective intelligence and enable a significant acceleration of innovation through the Internet. Soon, new technologies will allow us to communicate more effectively with computers and go beyond simple keyboards and mice.

However, we must be vigilant, because this new type of artificial intelligence could have harmful impacts on the humanity. We must act now to prevent these potential effects from getting out of hand. This is an important question that is being asked today and on which philosophers and legislators have begun to debate. We can imagine a day when computers manage our complex world, exchange ideas and even "reproduce" themselves. We must ask ourselves if this is desirable.

The combination of artificial and human intelligence offers a previously unimaginable potential and an acceleration of human knowledge even greater than that experienced in the last century. Eventually, this will produce a new form of intelligence that will be the symbiosis between living beings and artificial intelligence.

Attention science fiction writers, there may be material for you in this book. Enjoy your reading!

Artificial Intelligence

The Imitation Game

In his 1950 paper titled "Computing Machinery and Intelligence," Alan Turing, considered by many to be the father of artificial intelligence, asked if machines could think.

This question is still a frequent source of discussion, navigating the border between technology, philosophy, neuroscience, and theology. However, more than half a century ago, Turing proposed an indirect way to answer it through the famous Turing test.

Turing thought that to answer this question unambiguously, it was necessary to rephrase the question itself, clarifying or replacing the meaning of the words "think" and "machines": "Can a machine do what we, as thinking entities, can do?"

In other words, can a machine mimic or imitate a person? We can find the answer to this question in "the imitation game."

The test proposed by Turing takes the form of a game, with three players who are not in the same room together. An interrogator asks textual questions of a man and a woman to determine their gender based on their answers (a bit sexist as a game, one might say). However, here the man is asked to pretend to be a woman to complicate the game and make it harder to tell. Once the first game is over, a computer replaces the man, still with the role of pretending to be a woman. At the end, the human-machine performance in this imitation game is compared to describe the level of the artificial intelligence. In another version, the interrogator is alone in facing a computer in charge of convincing him he is human. The goal for the machine is not to give correct answers to the questions, but to provide answers that resemble those of a human would give.

We consider the Turing test having been passed when the evaluator cannot reliably distinguish the machine from the human player. The first program to pass was ELIZA, an artificial intelligence written by Joseph Weizenbaum in 1966. A similar program, Kenneth Colby's PARRY, passed this milestone in 1972. Nowadays, hundreds of chatbots are capable of deceiving human beings. Among them, ChatGPT.

Fundamentals First

ARTIFICIAL INTELLIGENCE (or AI) refers to the category of computing that seeks to mimic the functions of human intelligence within computer systems. These are programs that run on computers, and which include various methods, such as machine learning and deep learning, among others. To people outside the world of computers, this may sound threatening, as if machines could replace human intelligence. But that's a far cry from what AI is really for.

Throughout our lives, we learn and memorize new knowledge thanks to the billions of neurons in our brain. In the same way, AI applications use artificial neural networks to "learn" how to remember and recognize faces, texts, or ideas.

Unlike computers that simply repeat what programmers have dictated to them, AI applications can "self-program" by analyzing images, reading text, or listening to your voice. They can recognize the difference between a cat and a dog just by looking at thousands of images of these animals.

These applications are already many and well known. Some apps now available on smartphones can recognize your face and detect your emotions. You can now converse with your phone or dictate a message thanks to voice recognition algorithms.

But this technology can do even greater things. It can detect cancerous tumors more efficiently than a radiologist can. It can drive your car by itself, debate a particular subject, give its opinion on a legal ruling, or write newspaper articles from scratch.

Back to the Future

THE CONCEPT OF NON-living entities becoming intelligent beings have existed for a long time. Even the ancient Greeks had myths about robots, while Chinese and Egyptian engineers constructed automata.

In 1771, the *Gazette du Commerce* reported on a fascinating attraction that had been captivating audiences for over a year at the court of Vienna: an automaton that could play chess. The automaton was in the form of a mannequin with a mustache and turban, sitting in front of a small table with a chessboard on top. The mechanism was an optical illusion, concealing the real depth of the cabinet. The cabinet had a secret compartment where a real person could hide and control the dummy without being seen. The automaton played chess against human opponents, and thanks to the hidden human player's talent, it won most of its games. This Mechanical Turk was a remarkable feat of engineering and deception, fooling people into believing that a machine could play chess with human-like intelligence.

Although artificial intelligence can be traced back to attempts by classical philosophers to describe human thought as a symbolic system, the term "artificial intelligence" was coined in 1956 at a conference at Dartmouth College in Hanover, New Hampshire. MIT cognitive scientist Marvin Minsky and others at the conference were extremely optimistic about the future of AI (perhaps a little too much). In his view, the problem of creating "artificial intelligence" would be largely solved within a generation. As we'll see later, we were still a long way off.

But achieving an artificially intelligent being was not so simple. After a period that lasted from 1974 to 1980 and known as the "AI winter," the field was revived in the 1980s when the British government began funding it again, partly to compete with Japanese efforts.

The field went through another major winter from 1987 to 1993 (during my Ph.D.), which coincided with the collapse of the market for some of the first general-purpose computers and a reduction in government funding.

WHY CHATGPT IS A GAME-CHANGER

But the search resumed in 1997, when IBM's Deep Blue supercomputer became the first computer to beat Russian chess grandmaster Garry Kasparov. In 2011, the Watson computer won the TV game show "Jeopardy" by beating defending champions Brad Rutter and Ken Jennings.

However, it wasn't until recently that we have witnessed a breakthrough in the development of intelligent algorithms. This was in 2012, the third year of the annual ImageNet competition, which challenged teams to build computer vision systems that could recognize 1,000 objects, from animals to landscapes to people.

In the first two years, the best teams had failed to achieve even 75 percent accuracy. But in the third year, a group of three researchers (a professor and his students) suddenly surpassed that ceiling. They won the competition by a staggering 10% more precise. That professor was Geoffrey Hinton, and the technique they used is called deep learning.

In the fourth year of the ImageNet competition, almost all teams were using deep learning and achieving miraculous gains in accuracy. Soon, deep learning was applied to tasks beyond image recognition in a wide range of industries.

In 2019, for his seminal contributions to the field, Hinton was awarded the Turing Award, the equivalent of the Nobel Prize in computer science, alongside AI pioneers Yann LeCun and Yoshua Bengio.

Another big step that has enabled the rapid advancement of AI is the development of increasingly powerful computers.

Thanks to the exponential advancement of computer performance, specifically the use of graphics cards in video games, more and more interest has been shown in artificial intelligence and the development of increasingly complex models. These graphic cards, or GPU (for *Graphic Processing Unit*), can make parallel calculations and have proven to be very efficient for the learning process of neural networks, which can sometimes be long to calculate.

In 2012, Google connected 16,000 computer processors, gave them access to the Internet, and watched the machines learn on their own (by watching millions of randomly selected YouTube videos) how to identify ... cats. What may seem ridiculously simplistic is, in fact, an earth-shattering scientific breakthrough.

Despite the feat, which proved that deep learning programs were getting faster and more accurate, Google researchers knew it was just the beginning. Since then, Google, Facebook, Microsoft and almost every other tech giant have been in a deep learning gold rush, vying for the world's small pool of experts. Deep learning startups, funded by hundreds of millions of dollars in venture capital, are multiplying.

How It Works

ARTIFICIAL INTELLIGENCE algorithms are based on mathematical models based on the natural neural networks found in our brains. This type of network comprises specialized cells called neurons that exchange information with each other through axons. The axon or nerve fiber extends the neuron that carries the electrical signal from one cell to another.

When a child sees a cat for the first time, the neurons in his memory "record" this event by strengthening the links between certain neurons. During childhood, a human learns to recognize cats and associates them with the word "cat." This association becomes so strong that when we see another cat, we can immediately name it.

Artificial neural networks work on the same principle as their natural counterpart. They are represented by non-linear mathematical functions that simulate the natural reaction of neurons. These mathematical models are often graphically represented by circles interconnected by links. Each link has a weight which multiplies the output value of each circle.

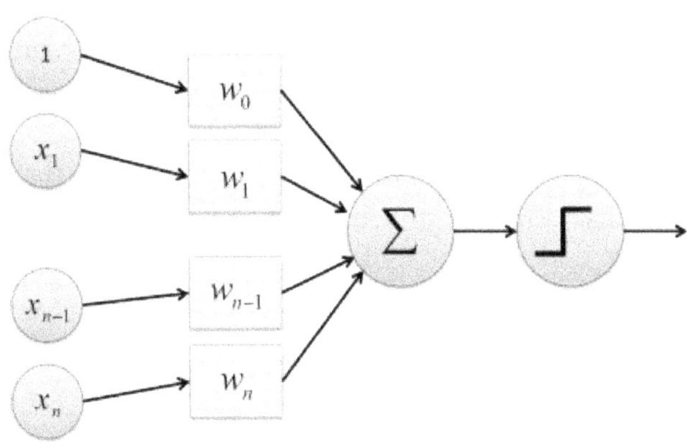

Basic neural network (Source: DeepAI)

IN A SIMPLE NETWORK, we will often have an input matrix representing the values at the input (e.g., cat image), an intermediate neuron layer and an "output layer" representing the class (or the word "cat").

During my time as a Ph.D. candidate, a fellow researcher in our department was conducting a study on the eyes of Drosophila, also known as fruit flies. Their research focused on modeling the neural networks of these tiny insects, specifically the neurons connected to their eyes. By using miniature probes, they recorded the electrical signals generated by the cells when exposed to bright light. With these measurements, they successfully recreated a portion of the fly's nervous system in the form of digital artificial neurons.

He noticed that one specificity of the eye of a fly is to recognize rapid movement. It is indeed thanks to this particularity that this insect can survive, because the quick detection of an approaching object, such as a horse's tail or a fly swatter, allows it to react quickly and to flee before being crushed.

In short, it is thanks to this kind of research that the first scientists were able to develop the foundations of artificial intelligence.

Generative AI

INTELLIGENCE IS NOT only used to recognize cats (fortunately!) A large part of AI research aims to develop applications that can generate original works.

WHY CHATGPT IS A GAME-CHANGER

Generative AI refers to the use of machine learning algorithms and artificial neural networks to create or generate new content. This content can be in the form of images, videos, music, text, or other forms of data.

Generative AI works by analyzing large amounts of existing data and learning the patterns and structures within it. It then uses this knowledge to generate new data that is like the original data, but not identical. We can do this in a variety of ways, such as by predicting the next word in a sentence, generating new images based on existing ones, or creating new music based on a particular style.

The applications of generative AI are vast and diverse, with potential uses in multiple industries. For instance, we can use generative AI to generate innovative artwork, produce music, or design new video games. It can aid designers in generating fresh product ideas, optimizing designs, or even creating new product concepts based on consumer preferences. We can also utilize generative AI to create chatbots or virtual assistants that can give humanlike responses to customer inquiries. In addition, it can generate synthetic medical images or simulate the effects of new medications on the human body.

Overall, generative AI is a rapidly developing field that has the potential to revolutionize the way we create and interact with data, leading to new opportunities and innovations in various fields.

ChatGPT

NATURAL LANGUAGE PROCESSING (NLP) has made significant progress in recent years, although understanding human language still poses challenges for AI. Reading and comprehending a word or a sentence requires not only knowledge of the language it is written in but also a basic understanding of the subject. Despite advancements in image recognition, NLP has not yet achieved the same level of success in understanding language and its nuances. Nonetheless, ongoing research and development in NLP continue to push the boundaries of AI language comprehension.

ChatGPT (short for "Chat Generative Pretrained Transformer") is a type of generative AI system that is based on the GPT (Generative Pretrained Transformer) architecture. It is a language model that has been trained on a massive amount of text data and can generate humanlike responses to user input.

ChatGPT works by using NLP techniques to analyze the user's input and generate a response that is appropriate to the context and intent of the conversation. The model can understand and process various types of language, including slang, idioms, and colloquial expressions.

This technology has a wide range of applications in various industries, including customer service, healthcare, education, and entertainment. It can create chatbots, virtual assistants, or other conversational AI systems that can give personalized and interactive experiences to users.

WHY CHATGPT IS A GAME-CHANGER

One of the major advantages of ChatGPT is its ability to adapt and learn from new data, making it a highly flexible and versatile solution for conversational AI. However, it is important to note that, like any AI system, ChatGPT has its limitations and may produce inaccurate or inappropriate responses in certain situations.

However, despite all the amazing progress in the world of AI in recent years, can we really speak of "intelligence" when we talk about these computer programs? What needs to be understood here is that ChatGPT did not think of it answers alone. It has in fact only repeated what is already on the web. People compare this type of technology to a "stochastic parrot" that is, it only regurgitates what the web already contains.

However, and this is the brilliant innovation is that unlike Google's search bots that roam the web to create a super knowledge index, ChatGPT can create links between knowledge and put it in context to refine its searches and produce more relevant answers.

A crucial differentiating factor of this novel technology is its utilization of context, setting it apart from earlier NLP methodologies. ChatGPT uses context in its answers by analyzing the user's previous messages and using them to infer the underlying context of the conversation. It does this by considering not only the words used in the current message but also the previous messages in the conversation.

For example, if the user asks, "What is the capital of France?" in one message and follows up with "What is the population of

Paris?" in the next message, ChatGPT can infer that the user is asking about France and its capital, Paris (and not Paris, Texas). It can then use this context to give a more relevant and accurate response to the second question.

Additionally, ChatGPT can understand and incorporate contextual information such as tone, sentiment, and topics. For example, if the user is expressing frustration or anger in their messages, ChatGPT can adjust its responses to be more empathetic and supportive. Similarly, if the conversation shifts to a different topic, ChatGPT can adapt its responses to stay on topic.

A Static World

THERE ARE STILL MANY things to discover in the fabulous field of AI. Most of the artificial intelligence methods developed so far are good enough to recognize objects or people from an image, so-called instantaneous events where you only need one image to recognize what it is. It is much more difficult to recognize events in time, such as dance movements or the sign language of the hearing impaired. This is called causality. These forms, which can be described as dynamic, require the analysis of a sequence of images in which one must recognize the objects (e.g., a dancer or hand movements) in each image, but also understand and characterize the trajectory of these objects and the context in which they evolve to identify them.

Let's take the example where we want to recognize which dance a couple is doing from a video sequence (salsa, waltz, disco, etc.). First, the artificial intelligence must recognize the two people in the images, their position in relation to each other, the movements of their feet, the position of their arms and the rhythm of their swing. In addition, it also interpreted the type of dance by recognizing the type of music based on the rhythm, the melody, or the type of instrument played. We can quickly see that to recognize something that seems so simple to us, we need to combine different specialized artificial neural networks to do the job. The human brain naturally uses the information interpreted by our different neural networks to do this task.

Recent research in AI for causality has focused on developing algorithms that can handle complex causal relationships, such as feedback loops and non-linear interactions. Deep learning has been used to develop models that can learn causal relationships from raw data with no explicit causal models. Other research has focused on developing techniques to learn causal models from observational data, using methods such as causal discovery and causal inference.

Overall, the field of AI for causality is still in its early stages, but it has the potential to have a significant impact on a wide range of fields, including healthcare, economics, and social science.

In the upcoming chapters, we will explore the challenge of precisely defining the concept of intelligence. I will endeavor to show a correlation between intelligence and the act of creation. Additionally, I will present a fresh categorization of intelligent systems that differs from the earlier classifications based on their functional types (mathematical, spatial, interpersonal, etc.). Instead, this new categorization will be based on their ability to interact and exchange information with other comparable systems. This approach will enable us to better situate our understanding of intelligence with both other living organisms and artificial intelligence. By utilizing this approach, I will show you how to engage with AI effectively to enhance our productivity and creativity.

Defining the Elusive

W e often associate the creative power of a person with his or her intelligence. Indeed, many inventions or works of art were created by men and women of exceptional intelligence or emotional sensitivity.

As stated in the Encyclopedia Britannica, we define human intelligence as "the mental quality that consists of the ability to learn from experience, adapt to new situations, understand and process abstract concepts, and use one's knowledge to manipulate one's environment." While this definition describes the attributes of intelligence, it does not answer the basic question that has plagued the minds of philosophers throughout the century: how does it work?

For centuries, people have tried to understand how human intelligence works. Over history, they quickly discovered that human beings were more advanced and intelligent than any other animal on earth. Homo sapiens could quickly establish himself at the top of the food chain, not by brute strength or speed but by intelligence and resilience, because, let's face it, Homo sapiens is not the most robust animal in the world. He has, however, shown by his ability to adapt to many situations quickly.

Many philosophers, such as Aristotle or Descartes, have tried to understand what characterizes human intelligence and what makes our species so superior and dominant compared to other animals. However, after having proposed many hypotheses trying to explain intelligence, we still cannot fully define and grasp what the concepts of intelligence, creativity or genius are.

The Soul, This Intangible Fabric

INTELLIGENCE IS OFTEN associated with the human soul. But although most philosophers acknowledge the existence of the human soul, there are differing views on its nature, its relationship to our bodies, and its purpose after death. There are those who believe that the soul is a material substance, others who claim that it is incorporeal. Some think that it is unquestionably linked to our body, others that it is dissociated from it. Finally, some believe that it dies with us and others maintain it is immortal.

Twenty-three hundred years ago, the famous Greek philosopher Aristotle first referred to something close to the idea of intelligence which he called "reason." Reason, according to him, was about the ability of humans to manage their passions, or, in other words, their ability to resist the urge of their instincts. This was what separated us from animals: humans were right, beasts did not.

Aristotle postulated that the body and the soul exist as facets of the same being. He suggests that the intellect is composed of two parts: one like matter (the passive intellect that one might associate with the body) and the other resembling the concept of the "soul" (which one might associate with the mind). Aristotle claims that intellect is separate from the body since it is in its nature essential and incorruptible. When the intellect is freed from the body, it appears as what it is and nothing more. It alone is immortal and without it, no thinking is possible.

Much later, in southern Italy, theologian, and philosopher Thomas Aquinas took Aristotle's ideas and reworked them to fit his Christian theological framework. Aquinas believed that the intellect made life on earth understandable by explaining things we do not experience directly, such as the notion of God and the creative idea. Like Aristotle, he believed that the rational soul of man was immortal. Man is by his very existence at the junction of two universes, "as a horizon of the corporeal and the spiritual." In man, there is not only a distinction between spirit and nature but also an intrinsic homogeneity of the two. Although his ideas were controversial for many centuries, his views became the official philosophy of the Roman Catholic Church and are still taught in Catholic schools today.

The concept of the soul is present in many major religions. In Judaism, it's believed that humans don't possess a soul but instead are a soul. When someone dies, they return to Sheol, a state of nothingness, until the time of resurrection. In Islam, there are three spiritual entities within a human: the soul, psyche, and spirit. The soul is an immortal substance that leaves the body upon death, while the spirit is the rational side that serves as the basis for all judgments. There being, or psyche, is made up of the union between the soul and spirit. In Hinduism, the soul can have various meanings such as the essential principle that organizes all living beings or the vital breath. It's believed that the soul survives by undergoing reincarnation into different bodies, including human, animal, or plant forms depending on the theory.

René Descartes, a 17th-century philosopher, believed in the duality of mind and body. According to Descartes, the soul is indivisible and immaterial, while the body is material and divisible. He believed that the soul is the source of consciousness and rational thought, whereas the body is the seat of sensations and passions. Descartes also emphasized the importance of the body in the human experience, stating that the body is essential for the expression of emotions and the experience of sensory perception. In contrast to the Christian view, which prioritizes the soul over the body, Descartes believed in the interdependence of the two, as a corpse cannot experience any sensations without the soul.

Spinoza goes further than Descartes and proposes that the body and the mind are the same but expressed in two ways. Born on November 24, 1632, in Amsterdam, Baruch Spinoza is a Dutch philosopher who occupies an important place in the history of philosophy. Spinoza rejects all divine transcendence and refers to nature as the source of all creation. He will therefore propose to study the nature of the body from the body itself, and not from thought or from the soul. With Spinoza, the seat of intelligence moves from the soul to the body. Spinoza's philosophy thus opened the way for science to explain what intelligence is.

In the 19th century, British naturalist, and paleontologist Charles Darwin revolutionized biology with his theories of evolution and natural selection. For Darwin, reason could be broken down into gradations, where some people have more and others less. The idea was based on his observations of evolution and how "mental powers" were greater, in more evolved species:

"[...] a high degree of intelligence is certainly compatible with complex instincts, and although actions, at first learned voluntarily, may soon, by habit, be performed with the rapidity and certainty of reflex action, it is not improbable that there is some interference between the development of free intelligence and that of instinct, the latter involving some inherited modification of the brain. Little is known of the functions of the brain, but we may perceive that as the intellectual powers develop, the different parts of the brain must be connected by very complex channels of very free intercommunication [...]" (Darwin, 1871)

The importance of Charles Darwin's contributions to the history of our understanding of intelligence and especially of the human brain cannot be overemphasized. With Darwin, we begin to wonder if the human soul and intelligence are not the result of natural and physical evolution, rather than emerging from a metaphysical or divine source.

Since the end of the 19th century, the advancement of science in the understanding of our body and especially of our brain have allowed us to question the very principle of the existence of the human soul. Recent knowledge about the functioning of the brain has changed our relationship with spirituality. Research in this field allows us to question the very essence of the soul as the seat of intelligence. Is the mind just matter arranged in neurons and molecules, directed by genes? In other words, can physicochemical phenomena explain our actions and thoughts only?

Measuring Intelligence

ALL THESE PHILOSOPHERS have proposed a definition of what intelligence is without really proving their hypothesis beyond any doubt. The nature and source of intelligence remain a nebulous and elusive concept.

However, the need to classify people into various categories has led some societies to categorize people based on a measure of their intelligence. This classification has allowed rulers (e.g., kings, lords, and governments) to have some leverage over their subjects and the general population.

Alfred Binet developed the first modern intelligence quotient (IQ) test in history in 1904 (1857–1911) and Théodore Simon (1873–1961). The French Ministry of Education had asked these researchers to develop a test that would distinguish mentally retarded children from normally intelligent but lazy children. The result was the Simon-Binet IQ test. This IQ test includes several components, such as logical reasoning, rhyming word association, and object naming.

The results of the IQ test, combined with the child's age, provide information about their intellectual development and whether they are ahead or behind other children. We calculate IQ as (mental age/chronological age) x 100. This test has been a tremendous success in both Europe and America.

Subsequently, others proposed improved versions of the Simon-Binet test. Based on this test and the Stanford-Binet test (the American version of the Simon-Binet test), American psychologist David Wechsler created a new measurement instrument. Like Binet, Wechsler believed that intelligence involved different mental abilities. Dissatisfied with the limitations of the Stanford-Binet test, he published his new intelligence test in 1955, known as the Wechsler Adult Intelligence Scale (WAIS).

When it was conceived, the IQ test offered a relatively quick and simple way to identify and sort individuals based on their intelligence, the latter of which is highly valued by society. In the United States and elsewhere, institutions such as the military and the police have used IQ tests to screen potential applicants. They have also set admission requirements for various institutions based on the results.

Along with the widespread use of IQ tests in the twentieth century, some argued their biology influenced a person's level of intelligence. Ethnocentrism and eugenicists, who considered intelligence and other social behaviors to be determined by race and biology, latched onto IQ tests. They pointed to the apparent discrepancies that these tests highlighted between ethnic minorities and whites or between low- and high-income groups.

Some have argued that these test results provide further evidence that socioeconomic and racial groups are genetically different from one another and that systemic inequalities are in part a by-product of evolutionary processes.

The results of the intelligence test used in the U.S. military were widely publicized and were analyzed by Carl Brigham, a Princeton University psychologist and founder of psychometrics, in a 1922 book entitled *A Study of American Intelligence*. Brigham applied meticulous statistical analysis to show that American intelligence was declining, claiming that increased immigration and racial integration were to blame. To remedy this problem, he advocated social policies to restrict immigration and prohibit racial mixing.

But in their darkest moments, IQ tests became a powerful means of excluding and controlling marginalized communities using empirical and scientific language. Proponents of eugenicist ideologies in the 1900s used IQ tests to identify "idiots," "imbeciles," and "feeble-minded" people. These were people, who the eugenicists believed threatened to dilute the white Anglo-Saxon genetic stock of America.

Because of these eugenicist arguments, many American citizens were sterilized. In 1927, an infamous U.S. Supreme Court ruling legalized the forced sterilization of developmentally disabled and "feeble-minded" citizens, who were often identified by their low IQ scores. This ruling, known as Buck v. Bell, resulted in the forced sterilization of over 65,000 people who were thought to have low IQs. Of course, the people who were forcibly sterilized because of Buck v. Bell were disproportionately poor or of color.

In the United States, forced sterilization based on IQ, criminality, or sexual deviance officially continued until the mid-1970s, when organizations such as the Southern Poverty

Law Center began filing lawsuits on behalf of those who had been sterilized. In 2015, the U.S. Senate voted to compensate living victims of government-sponsored sterilization programs.

IQ Does Not Tell the Entire Story

AT THE END OF WORLD War II, they tried over 100 Nazis in Nuremberg. Among those who tried were the "Nuremberg 21," some of the highest-ranking Nazi leaders.

After assessing their inherent personalities, the prosecutors had experts evaluate the intelligence of the 21 Nazi leaders by conducting IQ tests. The use of IQ tests is not uncommon in death penalty cases, as they can help determine whether the defendant is intellectually disabled and therefore not eligible for execution.

Bad or not, few suspected these leaders of being fools. And what is fascinating about this test is that it is the only known IQ test of an entire branch of the Nazi government leadership.

All of those tested showed above-average IQs. A few of them scored very high. The average of the 21 Nazi leaders was 128, nearly two standard deviations higher than the average person (the average IQ being 100).

There is a bitter irony in this, for IQ tests were just another mechanism used by the Nazis to kill and sterilize nearly half a million people. And their high scores went a long way toward serving their egos.

Thus, the quest to understand intelligence has been a controversial topic throughout history. Despite the considerable interest in the subject, there is still disagreement about the components of intelligence. In addition to the question of how to define intelligence, the debate continues to this day whether precise measurements are even possible.

A Physical Investigation

WHEN ALBERT EINSTEIN died in 1955, pathologist Thomas Harvey made a decision that would change the course of his life: he shaved off the physicist's unruly hair, stripped him of his scalp and opened his skull to remove the precious gray matter.

For over 20 years, this event was never heard of again. All indications are that, after being kicked out of Princeton Hospital, Thomas Harvey took Einstein's brain with him ... in his suitcase.

In 1978, young journalist Steven Levy knocked on his office door. According to him, "He took a box with Costa Cider written on it and pulled out two glass jars filled with formaldehyde, in which were floating dozens of small cubes," a few weeks after the removal. Thomas Harvey had indeed cut the brain into some 240 pieces.

Solicited from all sides after the publication of Steven Levy's article, Thomas Harvey sent slices and cubes of the brain to researchers around the world.

WHY CHATGPT IS A GAME-CHANGER

After having scrutinized and probed the defunct neurons in their smallest ramifications, most scientists did not publish the fruit of their research, for the simple reason that they had found nothing interesting. Three of the scientists noticed something, however. Marian Diamond, a neuroanatomist at the University of California, Berkeley, wrote in 1985 in the journal *Neurology* that "the ratio of glial cells to neurons is higher in Einstein's parietal lobes than in the average of the 11 control brains analyzed." Dr. Britt Anderson of the University of Alabama's Department of Neurology believes that "Einstein's frontal cortex was more densely packed with neurons than the control brains." He published these unconvincing results in *Neuroscience Letters* in 1996.

It was neuropsychologist Sandra Witelson of the G. DeGroote School of Medicine at McMaster University in Hamilton who wrote the most widely discussed article on the subject in the prestigious medical journal *The Lancet* in 1999: "Einstein's exceptional brain. His parietal lobes are larger because of the configuration of the Sylvian fissure, which meets the postcentral sulcus." In other words, in Einstein's brain, the surface area of a brain region that plays a crucial role in visuospatial integration and mathematical ideation is larger, since the long crevice that normally binds it is in a unique position than normal.

Today, no one doubts Einstein's genius. His conception and modeling of the physical world revolutionized an entire area of experimental science. The most astonishing thing is that he developed his entire theory of relativity based solely on his intuitions.

Despite these discoveries concerning the development of certain parts of his brain, we can easily deduce that he had the mental capacity to develop his theory. But was he more intelligent than anyone else? Or did he have an extraordinary ability to manipulate abstract and mathematical concepts?

Gray Plastic

MARIAN DIAMOND WAS the first woman to graduate from the Department of Anatomy at UC Berkeley in the early 1950s. A decade later, she was to be at the origin of a true scientific revolution in the still-young field of neuroscience.

At the time, they did not believe that the brain could change significantly during life. There was a consensus in the scientific community that it was only our genes that determined the structure of our brain. But Marian Diamond would demonstrate the opposite. She raised rats in an enriched environment, meaning in large cages with lots of people and objects to explore, and compared their brains to those of other rats raised in an impoverished environment (alone, in a small cage, with no objects). By observing slices of their respective cortexes under a microscope, Diamond noted significant differences, particularly in the young rats raised in an enriched environment: their cortex was 6% thicker!

The research conducted by Marian Diamond and others has revealed that the human brain is not static at birth but rather possesses the ability to adapt and rewire itself based on an individual's experiences throughout their lifetime. This remarkable capacity for change and adaptation is known as "plasticity," drawing an analogy to the malleability of materials.

For example, following a knee injury, we can condition our nervous system to become more reactive or train other muscles to compensate for weaker ones. Similarly, we can condition or train the creative and analytical part of our brain to become more efficient. The trick is to know-how.

Fifty Shades of Gray

OTHER RESEARCHERS HAVE tried to give a broader definition of intelligence. According to Harvard Professor Howard Gardner's theory of multiple intelligence, we do not possess only one type of intelligence, but eight different forms.

1. **Logical-mathematical intelligence**: People who are gifted in calculation, who like to solve logical problems, and who constantly analyze the causes and consequences of phenomena around them. They like to categorize and put in order, and love puzzles, brainteasers, strategy games, and deduction games.

2. **Verbo-linguistic intelligence**: Those who are gifted in using language. It is present in writers, poets, lawyers, or great orators.

3. **Spatial intelligence**: This is the intelligence of people who are skilled at representing precise and complex mental images. This form of intelligence is particularly developed in geographers, painters, designers, pilots, navigators, and architects, for example.

4. **Interpersonal intelligence**: People who like to learn,

to improve, to question themselves and to be self-critical. It is also part of emotional intelligence, along with interpersonal intelligence listed below. It is not surprising that many people who have developed this type of intelligence are passionate about personal development and love to learn many things by themselves. These people often have a love of exploration, research, or writing and seek to increase their knowledge and skills.

5. **Kinesthetic or bodily intelligence**: Those who enjoy learning through physical sensations. Most often, they love sports or theatrical expression and have difficulty learning by sitting in a classroom, listening to theoretical concepts. This type of intelligence is particularly developed in athletes, dancers, and all professions that require excellent control of the body and its movements.

6. **Interpersonal intelligence**: People who can empathize and guess at the intentions, moods, motivations, and feelings of others and respond appropriately. They make talented politicians, speakers, teachers, consultants, salespeople, or mediators, for example.

7. **Musical/rhythmic intelligence**: Those who are good at memorizing melodies, harmonizing sounds, and recognizing rhythms. These people like everything that has to do with music and understand the influence of certain rhythms on our emotions. They particularly developed this intelligence in musicians, musicologists, sound engineers, or poets, for example.

8. **Naturalistic intelligence**: People who can differentiate between living beings and who are sensitive to the characteristics of the surrounding world. These people like to observe nature and have a privileged relationship with it. They are also very aware of ecosystems, ecology, the organization of living beings, etc. This intelligence is particularly developed in botanists, biologists, or zoologists, for example.

If we refer to this definition of intelligence, we can understand that Einstein had a certain type of intelligence. He had an above-average logical, mathematical, and spatial intelligence. However, he probably had an average level of interpersonal and even musical intelligence (he played the violin).

People on the autism spectrum may perform at a very high cognitive level in specific areas where they spend a lot of time and energy. Some may have phenomenal memories, do calculations quickly, or learn music in no time. Studies have shown that people with autism have different intelligence than the average person.

Uncertainty

ALTHOUGH THERE MAY be different definitions of intelligence proposed by various theorists, recent conceptualizations tend to suggest that intelligence comprises the following abilities:

1. **Learning from experience**: the acquisition,

retention, and use of knowledge are an important component of intelligence.

2. **Recognizing problems**: To apply knowledge, people must be able to identify potential problems that need to be addressed.

3. **Problem solving**: People must then be able to use this knowledge and experience to find a useful solution to a problem that they have noticed in the world around them.

Intelligence involves a variety of mental abilities, including logic, memory, reasoning, problem solving, and planning. While intelligence is one of the largest and most studied, it is also one of the most controversial.

By remembering the history of the philosophy of our thought, we quickly notice the complexity of defining intelligence. At what level can we talk about exceptional intelligence or genius? Should we speak of multiple types of intelligence or of a single intelligent form?

In this categorization of intelligence types, one must ask whether one can have greater skills in logic and mathematics and be deficient in other aspects, such as interpersonal intelligence. Can intelligence really be categorized or is it part of an interrelated whole?

First, let's get one thing straight: the myth that we only use a fraction of our brain is false. Nature hates things that are useless. Let's be clear: all our brain cells are used. If they weren't, they would die. Most of them are obviously used for what I would call low-level (or reptilian) services, such as breathing, walking, vision. It is important to understand that the human body is an extremely complex system governed by a multitude of equally complex intelligent control systems. Only part of our brain contributes to our thoughts and to what is called consciousness.

In the next chapter, I will discuss how our species, Homo sapiens, has stood out so much from other animal species and what conditions have helped us dominate the world.

Standing Out

A Systemic Approach

Philosophers today, both professionals and amateurs, often identify as humanists. Humanism is a philosophical approach that emphasizes human values and concerns, with the belief that humans are the ultimate source of meaning and value in the world. This contrasts with the medieval concept of theocentrism, which placed God at the center of human existence and understanding. The humanist approach holds that individuals have the ability and responsibility to determine their own beliefs, values, and actions based on reason, empathy, and compassion for others.

Personally, I am a follower of "relationalism." At its core, it posits that objects and forms in the universe do not exist in isolation, but rather exist in relation to other entities, and that their properties and characteristics are shaped by these relationships. This way of thinking emphasizes the interconnectedness and interdependence of things in the world and suggests that we cannot fully understand anything without understanding its relationships with other things.

We can find relationalism in various philosophical traditions, including process philosophy, phenomenology, and existentialism. We often contrast it with individualism, which emphasizes the independence and autonomy of individual entities.

In relationalism, we see everything as part of a larger network of relationships, and there is no inherent or fixed identity or essence to any object or form. This approach can have significant implications for various areas of philosophy, including metaphysics, ethics, and epistemology.

Overall, this philosophy offers a perspective that challenges the traditional view of entities as isolated and self-contained and highlights the importance of context and interdependence in shaping things in the universe.

An ecosystem is a good example of relationalism. In an ecosystem, all living organisms, such as plants, animals, and microorganisms, depend on each other for survival. They form a complex network of relationships, where energy and nutrients are constantly exchanged. Even nonliving things like water, sunlight, and soil play a crucial role in shaping the ecosystem and its inhabitants. Each element is connected and interdependent, and any change in one part of the ecosystem can have a significant impact on the rest of the system.

This interconnectedness and interdependence of all the distinct elements of the ecosystem mean that changes to one part of the system can have significant effects on other parts of the system. For instance, the removal of a keystone species, such as a top predator, can have cascading effects on the entire ecosystem.

WHY CHATGPT IS A GAME-CHANGER

Moreover, interactions between basic elements of a system can produce behaviors or reactions that are not found in each element. Each living being is composed of cells whose individual functionality is trivial and simple, but when put into a system that is the animal or the plant, produces different behaviors and interactions. Biological cells only make sense when they enter a relationship with others. The whole is greater than the sum of its parts. One plus one equals three (you see my point).

The same principle generally applies to political, economic, and social systems. A society is a collection of human beings who interact to protect and help each other (or so we hope).

For example, in economic systems, there are many relationships between distinct entities, such as businesses, individuals, governments, and other organizations. For example, businesses rely on customers to buy their products or services, and customers rely on businesses to offer goods and services they need. Governments regulate the economic activities of businesses and individuals, and they also collect taxes that help fund public services.

Moreover, economic systems are often intertwined with other social, political, and environmental systems, and changes in one system can affect the others. For example, economic activities can impact the environment and natural resources, while environmental factors, such as natural disasters or climate change, can have economic implications.

Intelligence, like these systems, can be described by a series of interactions between various sensory brain systems. Organisms consist of various tissues and components that are all intricately interconnected, either directly or indirectly. Our body systems, such as our heart, hands, and stomach, interact through the transmission of nerve impulses to our brain, facilitated by the nervous system.

The brain and the spinal cord constitute the central nervous system, capable of integrating information, controlling motor skills, and ensuring cognitive functions. The brain is made up of different lobes, each with its own function. The frontal lobe is the place for reasoning, language, and voluntary motor coordination. The parietal lobe, located behind the frontal lobe, is the seat of awareness of the body and its surrounding space. The temporal lobe, located on the left side, is the center of hearing, memory, and emotions.

Moreover, each living being can even be subdivided into several intelligent subsystems. For example, the human brain has several areas that fulfill a specific role. Some areas, such as the cerebellum, collect all the information transmitted by the sensory system, the spinal cord, and other parts of the brain. It also plays the role of regulating motor movements. Other areas of the brain are related to language, vision, and listening.

The left hemisphere performs all tasks related to logic, such as science and mathematics. For example, in a discussion (which involves the language function) or when listening to a teacher, the left hemisphere records and assimilates all the transmitted information. The left hemisphere is in control of the right side of the body.

The right hemisphere is our "creative brain." It is involved in daydreaming and imagination. You use this part of your brain when you draw or use your creativity. As you can guess, the right hemisphere oversees the left side of the body.

Some of these areas, which I will call intelligent subsystems, address information through nerve links, but others use indirect means. In general, it can be said that people who can exchange easily between these zones have a greater capacity for creation and innovation.

Animal intelligence is defined by the nature of the interactions between the various components of the organism and the complexity of the information exchanges in the systemic context. For instance, the cells of the eye capture light and send the information to the visual cortex, behind the brain, via the optic nerves. The cortex interprets the electrical impulses before transmitting the data to other areas of the brain for further analysis. This allows us to recognize faces or appreciate sunsets. Therefore, intelligence is closely linked to the eye-nerve-brain system and the different organs that connect them to the external environment. An eye on its own cannot convey emotions while looking at a masterpiece painting. Similarly, the brain alone cannot respond without the eyes. Intelligence can only exist in the interaction between different organs, which is essential to connect them to the outside world.

In this definition, it is difficult to identify a single focus of intelligence, but rather a set of systems composed of tissues, nerves, and cells that capture light, sounds, and vibrations and memorize them and interpret the signals.

Does this mean that intelligence can be defined as a simple nervous reaction to external stimuli? In principle, yes, and here's why. If we define an intelligent system as a set of basic nervous structures connecting our organs to the external world, we can assume that any nervous reaction, ranging from the simple pain reaction to being hit to the wonderment before a great painter's work, is a manifestation of intelligence. However, the number of nervous interactions that are involved in the appreciation of a work of art is millions of times greater than when reacting to pain.

Indeed, according to this definition, we can define intelligence not in terms of IQ or level of intelligence, but instead in levels of complexity. We can define intelligence on a continuous spectrum based on the complexity of the interactions that living beings, machines, and computers can engage in.

Is it possible to define a threshold level of complexity beyond which we can classify the so-called intelligent beings and the others? Probably, but I think that an inclusive model without boundaries allows for a better understanding of what intelligence is. By not categorizing the levels of complexity of intelligence and by inserting them in a continuum, we avoid segregating living beings or men between each other. In human history, attempts to categorize intelligence by dividing white men and men of color or men and women has led to unjust and repressive social discrimination.

The Result of Evolution or Society?

IF WE DEFINE INTELLIGENCE according to eight different types as described in the previous chapter, this will not represent levels of intelligence, but, rather high-level abilities or specialized functions that our brain can do and that allow us to distinguish ourselves from other animals.

However, some of these abilities are superior in animals. For example, a dog can detect and identify scents far beyond that of a human. A hawk can recognize small animals in motion much more easily than a human.

On the other hand, humans have a much greater capacity for creation and adaptation than any other animal. This capacity has allowed us to rise to the top of the food chain during our evolution.

Why then are we so dominant as a species on Earth? What makes us different from animals and allows us to build cathedrals to the glory of God? And why are we the only ones who can benefit from these abilities?

In my opinion, the major difference comes from our ability to create and innovate which contribute to its resilience. Of course, we have already observed some animals being innovative, such as crows using stones to break eggs they have stolen or monkeys taking twigs to extract ants hidden in a rotten tree trunk. However, this doesn't compare with what humans have created.

It is exactly this unique ability of humans to create, invent and model the world abstractly that fascinates me. Each one of us has a creative potential that is gained. This potential is the fruit of millions of years of evolution and has allowed us to become what we are today: Homo sapiens.

Despite our well-intentioned egalitarian principles, we are not all born equal (at least at this level). Some people have superior creative abilities in certain fields, such as music or mathematics. One need only think of child prodigies such as Mozart and Beethoven, or Blaise Pascal, the mathematician. However, although a child may be born with extraordinary innate abilities, only a tiny fraction of them have left their mark on history. These innate abilities, programmed into our brains at random or by genetic constraints, do not represent the full extent of human intelligence.

However, although this innate condition is necessary, it is not sufficient. The ability to create and invent largely depends on our experiences, family environment, and education. Most of the men and women who have made their mark on history had an innate ability that may have been above average, yet what shaped them was their experience. Without this experience, their brains would not have developed in such a way as to create and invent new ideas that have revolutionized the world.

Mozart composed some of the most beautiful music in history, which is played over 200 years after his death (how many artists today will be able to boast of being played 200 years from now?) This exceptional artist certainly had extraordinary musical and spatial abilities, but what forged his intelligence was his relationship with his father, who pushed him to study music, and with the society of the time, which adulated talented artisans. It is worth considering whether Mozart would have achieved the same level of success and intelligence if he had been born in a different period or societal context. Therefore, Mozart's intelligence was not solely determined by his cognitive capacities but also by his relationships and environment.

Both Henri Poincaré and Albert Einstein shared the belief that scientific ideas and theories are products of free and creative thought, rather than simply derived from logical deductions based on empirical data. They recognized scientific theories are not predetermined by innate or gained cognitive structures, but rather emerge through a process of imaginative construction. This creative process allows for the emergence of new ideas that cannot be fully explained or predicted by existing knowledge, highlighting the importance of intellectual freedom and imagination in scientific inquiry.

I hold both Henri Poincaré and Albert Einstein in high esteem, but I must respectfully disagree with their perspective. From my point of view, personal experience plays a significant role in the process of discovery, even if one is not fully conscious of it. The act of uncovering new ideas is influenced by accumulated knowledge, personal experiences, and innate conditions, with each factor contributing to varying degrees.

A research group in France (Creapro) attempted to understand the creative processes of various groups, such as students, artists, engineers, and scientists. They discovered that there is not one but a plurality of creative processes, and that this process is not continuous but highly non-linear, meaning that one may follow a procedure like the scientific process, yet ideas may arise unexpectedly at any stage of the process. The work has also highlighted that the creative process is not yet fully understood and that several paths are possible and may depend on one's experience.

Growing and Creating

FROM THE MOMENT OF our birth, our memory is continuously activated by the influx of information and experiences. At first, these experiences are emotional, such as experiencing love or anger. Later, language allows us to convey more specific concepts, such as "I'm hungry" or "What's for dinner?" (Mostly during the teenage years). We realize that if we just had language, transferring knowledge from one generation to another would be quite limited.

Then, we go to school and learn how to read and write. We then learn thousands of things that we never thought of before. Thanks to writing, we can memorize a phenomenal quantity of new concepts that we could not yet imagine. We learn the Earth is round and that it revolves around the Sun, even if we have never been to space.

We are accustomed to believing that everything we read in books is true. Some who continue to learn also begin to question this knowledge. But it doesn't matter, because all this knowledge, whether true or false, is necessary to create.

We continue to learn and memorize things that enrich our minds. The older we get, the more our experiences enrich our knowledge and help us structure it. We learn how to drive a car, to love music or fine wines and to appreciate the smile of children. All these experiences define us and shape our personality.

Thomas Edison, inventor of the electric light bulb, gramophone, and direct current electricity, must have been a child of average intelligence during his childhood. It was during his adult years that he developed the full potential of his creative brain. He also showed that creation and invention occur by following a methodical and scientific process most of the time. To create the incandescent light bulb, he had to test thousands of different materials (over 6,000) for the bulb's filament before finding the right one. Anecdotally, although tungsten is used in contemporary light bulbs (before the advent of LED bulbs), the material that worked best, was bamboo.

The Winning Conditions

1) In my point of view, we can claim that the capacity of creation and invention in living beings is conditioned by three principles: the ability to communicate through advanced language and writing.

2) The ability to change our environment.

3) Simple motivations, such as the fear of dying and the will to survive, or more complex ones, such as wanting to solve a mathematical problem.

OF ALL THE LIVING SPECIES on earth, only humans have all three. Some animals, such as elephants and dolphins, have memories superior to those of humans, but do not have limbs that allow them to modify or manufacture anything. Monkeys have hands like those of humans, but their language is not advanced enough to exchange ideas and collaborate on creations.

It is not clear how humans have developed such an advanced language compared to other living things. The fact is that we are the only living species that can produce such a wide variety of sounds to communicate, which allows us to exchange ideas. It is likely that the first humans did not have a very elaborate vocabulary, but that language evolved through the need to live in society.

During the early days of human civilization, knowledge was passed down from one generation to another through oral tradition. Generally, oral tradition served two primary purposes. The first was to transmit historical information in the form of myths and legends. The second was to educate and govern the younger generation by imparting customs and practices. In the oral tradition, cultural transmission was often accomplished through storytelling and songs, as they were easier to remember and pass on to the next generation.

WHY CHATGPT IS A GAME-CHANGER

The amount of information that could be transmitted from one generation to the next was limited until the Sumerians invented writing. The remains of the temples in the cities of Uruk and Lagash, which are in present-day Iraq, contain the first evidence of writing, dating back to 3,300 years BC. The Sumerians used reeds with sharp edges to inscribe signs onto clay tablets.

The earliest examples of writing are pictographs used by temple officials to keep track of the city's grain and animal supplies, which in large Sumerian urban centers such as Ur were large enough that counting by memory was unreliable.

Writing made it much easier to pass on knowledge from one generation to the next. When the ancient Mesopotamians settled on the farms surrounding the first cities, life became a little more complicated. Farming required expertise and detailed record-keeping, both of which led directly to the invention of writing and mathematics, historians say.

Unfortunately, from ancient times until recently, reading and writing were not for the masses. Daily life in Mesopotamia and Egypt was time-consuming, so writing became a specialized profession, usually reserved for members of the elite. The valued scribes of ancient Mesopotamia were even depicted in art wearing cuneiform writing implements (much like a set of chopsticks) on their belts as a sign of importance. In most societies, literacy remained a privilege of the male aristocracy until the nineteenth century, when public education became widespread throughout the world.

Without language and writing, human knowledge would still be at the same point and innovation would not be possible, no matter how big our brain is. The first man who found a way to create fire with stones was able to pass his invention on to the next generation through language and oral tradition. Without this, we would still wonder how to heat our soup today.

The second condition for creation is the ability to change or adapt to the environment. Let's face it, if humans had wings instead of hands, our achievements would be much less impressive.

Man has two hands which allow him to complete a multitude of actions. Each hand has five fingers: the thumb, the index, the middle finger, the ring finger, and the little finger. The hand has twenty-seven bones, and a multitude of muscles attached to it.

These hands are very evolved in humans, and they are mainly used, to catch objects, but are also a means of expression and essential for the sense of touch. Scientists believe that without the evolution of the hand as we know it today, man could not have evolved in this way.

It has been known for many years that vertebrate limbs, including our arms and legs, have fish fins as their ancestors. The evolution that led to the appearance of limbs, and particularly the appearance of fingers in vertebrates, reflects a change in the body associated with a change in habitat, the transition from aquatic to terrestrial environments.

The original savanna hypothesis has long been the most accepted and taught theory. In accord with this theory, a man's ancestor would have learned to walk because the forest would become savanna in East Africa. Apart from the fact that there would have been no more trees to climb on, standing would have had multiple advantages, such as allowing for the transportation of tools or weapons imposed by the nomadic life of the savanna, and which indirectly improved the dexterity of our hands.

Finally, in addition to the ability to communicate and transform things, the main reason that drives an intelligent being to create is linked to its intrinsic motivation: survival. We can easily imagine that innovation appeared in humans out of necessity. Their ability to communicate and manipulate objects enabled them to create weapons that allowed them to hunt and therefore to survive. Moreover, the omnipresent predators and enemies forced them to create techniques of protection and war.

The sedentary lifestyle of man has allowed him to create communities, villages, and eventually cities. This socialization allowed us to exchange much more often with our fellow men. Through the creation of social groups, humans were able to protect themselves together, and the need to survive was able to give way to other necessities, such as trade, leisure, and the arts.

Trade between people of different villages created the conditions for innovations such as money and mathematics. The enrichment of some allowed them to stimulate artistic creation.

Lorenzo de Medici was one of the first patrons of the arts. Also known as "The Magnificent," he was born in Florence in 1449 and was one of the most famous and revered members of the Medici family. He played a key role in the political games of Italy and in the cultural life of Florence and was one of the chief patrons of the Florentine Renaissance. He allowed artists such as Leonardo da Vinci, Raphael, and Michelangelo to shine by innovating in their art. His fascinating story and that of his family deserves to be better known.

As we observe numerous examples, it becomes evident that the innovative aspect that sets humans apart from other organisms is largely attributed to socialization, which has facilitated the exchange of ideas among individuals. Our thoughts are no longer solely influenced by our individual experiences but also by our interactions with others. With the help of socialization, human intelligence has advanced to another level.

The Dynamics of Innovation

AS WE HAVE SEEN PREVIOUSLY, the human brain is made up of various intelligent systems, each with a specific function. Creation or innovation occurs when there is an exchange of information directly or indirectly between these different areas. The continuous exchange of this nervous information feeds the right side of the brain, the seat of creativity.

One might think that innovation cannot be attributed solely to a random process resulting from the interaction of various intelligent systems. The exchange of ideas is influenced by both intrinsic and extrinsic constraints. Intrinsic constraints refer to the internal capabilities of each system, while external constraints can be factors such as fear, pleasure, or social pressures. These constraints can both drive us to create and inhibit our desires.

By internal or intrinsic constraints, I mean all the mental limitations of an individual. These limitations can come from a lack of education or a lesser ability to memorize events and can also be limited by a lack of experience. It is through experience and the acquisition of knowledge that people build an individual memory that fuels creation.

External constraints are all the elements that inhibit individuals from exercising the process of creation and exchange of ideas. It is well known that during the Middle Ages, the Church, and the monarchies forced individuals to live according to a certain morality that did not value innovation at all, except perhaps in the arts. Moreover, reading and writing, which allow one to seek knowledge without experiencing it, were reserved for the elite. Other socioeconomic factors, such as the standard of living or family situations, can come into play and inhibit the essential motivation to create.

In the next chapter, I will attempt to show a link between intelligence and creation. I will also propose a new categorization of intelligent systems, not by its types of functionalities (mathematical, spatial, interpersonal, etc.) as described earlier, but according to their capacity to exchange information with other similar systems. This will allow us to better position our intelligence with other living beings and to artificial intelligence.

The Product of Intelligence

Imagination, the Muse of Creativity

Imagination is intrinsic to our inner life. One could even say that it makes up a "second universe" in our heads. We invent animals and events that don't exist, rewrite history with alternative outcomes, imagine social and moral utopias, revel in fantasy art, and ponder both what we could have been and what we could become. Animators like Walt Disney and the folks at Pixar Studios are masters of the art of imagination, but they are only creating a public version of our private, everyday lives. So why is imagination so little analyzed by philosophers, psychologists, and scientists?

Aristotle described the imagination as the human faculty of producing, memorizing, and recalling the mental images we form of the world. Even our sleep is fed by the dreams of our involuntary imagination. Immanuel Kant, an 18th century German philosopher, considered the imagination as a synthesis of the senses and of our understanding of the world. Although there are many differences between the philosophies of Aristotle and Kant, the latter agrees that the imagination is "a faculty of unconscious synthesis that brings together sense perceptions and binds them into coherent representations with real dimensions." In other words, imagination is a mental faculty that mediates between the particularities of the senses (for example, "bright blue colors") and our feelings and perceptions (for example, the judgment that "the blue windows in this painting are beautiful").

It is perhaps not surprising that philosophers and cognitive theorists have a rather dry view of the imagination, and our everyday ideas about imagination are not much better. Like the ancient Greeks, we still think of our own creativity as a muse that descends upon us, a kind of spiritual possession or miraculous madness that flooded Vincent Van Gogh and John Lennon, but just trickles down to you and me.

We have romanticized creativity so much that we have ended up with an impenetrable mystery in our heads. We may no longer literally believe in the possession of a muse, but we have not yet replaced the "mysterious" conception of imagination with a better one. This mysterious perception of imagination is vague and obscure, but it at least captures the off-center psychological state of creativity.

The "Cyberquanta"

SINCE MY CHILDHOOD, I have always been fascinated by the theories of physics and the history of physicists. My heroes were Newton and Einstein. Later, I studied the concepts of theoretical physics and understood the beauty of these models in the splendor of mathematics. These pioneers completely redefined our understanding of the universe, and their theories led philosophers to revise the classical models of the ancient Greeks. Quantum theory, for example, has allowed us to question the very foundations of the universe's existence.

WHY CHATGPT IS A GAME-CHANGER

One might think that Albert Einstein won his only Nobel Prize for his work on general relativity, but this is not the case. Instead, they rewarded him for his work in physical optics and for his explanation of the "photoelectric" effect, the emission of electrons by a material subjected to the action of light. On this occasion, he developed the concept of "grains" of light, which were later named "quanta" or "photons."

It was at this point that quantum physics took off. Light could be defined as an intangible and immaterial wave, but also as an elementary particle like electrons and protons. This wave-particle duality, which annoyed Einstein, was taken up by other famous physicists such as Louis de Broglie, Niels Bohr, and many others, and led to the development of quantum physics, a revolutionary theory that was fundamental to the development of modern electronic systems and computers.

The physicist and philosopher Erwin Schrödinger illustrates through a famous thought exercise an essential characteristic of quantum mechanics, that of the existence of particles. Imagine a closed box in which a cat is enclosed. Next to the cat, there is a dish filled with poisoned milk. There is a 50% chance that the cat will drink the milk and another 50% that it will not touch it. After a certain amount of time, is the cat dead or is it still alive? According to the principles of quantum mechanics, if we don't investigate the box, the cat is both alive and dead at the same time. The two states are superimposed. It is only by opening the box that we can determine its state.

According to the principles of quantum theory, the location of a particle is initially represented by a probability wave until an observation or measurement is performed. Once observed, the particle is then described by a specific and precise value. This means that a particle's existence and definition are dependent on its interaction with the observer or measuring devices.

Einstein was very reluctant to accept this concept. He could not admit that a thing could not exist, even if it was not observed. He kept challenging his physicist friend Niels Bohr by proposing theoretical experiments resulting from his thoughts. Each time, Bohr found the flaw in his friend's reasoning and thus refuted Einstein's objections to the quantum theory. However, despite his objections, the quantum theory has imposed itself by its understanding of the infinitely small.

This is in line with the systemic concept I introduced earlier, which extrapolates this idea into the general definition of existence: what defines something is directly linked to its interactions. Knowledge becomes an idea when it interacts. Like a light wave, knowledge is transmitted from one intelligent system to another imprecisely in the form of electric waves (neurons), sound waves (speech) or light waves (writing). It is when these ideas interact that ideas and inventions become concrete and defined. Just as the wave-particle duality of light, the duality of knowledge and ideas is equally valid.

While you may think my comparison to quantum physics is overstated, it provides a useful framework for appreciating the significance of interactions between intelligent systems during the design process. Intelligent systems can store and organize diverse knowledge and concepts, but it is the interplay between these elements that facilitates the emergence of novel creations, inventions, or discoveries. Ultimately, the ideas and works that we conceive arise from the deliberate interactions between our thoughts.

In a certain way, the creation, or the invention is determined to follow imposing a hypothesis or an experiment which represents the measure. It only takes shape if it is fixed by an idea. Without creation, invention, or discovery, knowledge would be useless. In fact, it would not **exist**.

The Creative Process

THROUGHOUT HISTORY, we can observe a correlation between periods of high human creativity and the instinct to survive. The earliest human inventions, such as fire, spears, and arrows, were primarily driven by the need to survive winter and obtain food. Similarly, times of brilliant innovation have often been linked to wars and revolutions. During the Middle Ages, artistic and martial inventions were under the control of the Church and the sovereigns. The Church's dogmatic beliefs imposed on citizens often made it nearly impossible to think differently, which severely hindered innovators' aspirations.

In theory, one could characterize the propensity for a human to create by certain extrinsic parameters which are beyond our control, such as the need to survive or the type of society in which we live. However, if we ignore these external constraints, we can define a certain number of rules and procedures that allow us to create. These are what we might call intrinsic or human-specific parameters.

In the following section, we will begin by describing how humans can create and generalize concepts to generalize these methods to other types of so-called intelligent systems such as computers.

Knowledge is the Basis

INNOVATION IS ABOVE all a question of knowledge. Culture and the experience that we gain throughout our lives are part of this knowledge. It is important to know that innovation or creation is usually about combining different notions or knowledge. We must therefore make sure we have enough knowledge to feed off on.

When I talk about knowledge, I don't mean technical knowledge in a specific field of science, but I include general knowledge, like other scientific fields or artistic ones like music, dance, or literature. This general knowledge essentially allows us to feed our brain with new ideas, but also helps us to structure our thoughts. Our experiences and even the games we play during our childhood also have a big role in this process. They allow us to observe and experiment with things in nature and with other people's behaviors, and to establish a list of possible or unlikely interactions. It is by playing with these types of relationships and knowledge that new things can be created.

Most of the great minds of this world have had passions other than the one that made them famous. Albert Einstein was a music lover and violinist in his spare time. It is said that one day Albert Einstein was playing a quartet with George Enesco, the famous Italian composer, but when he couldn't keep up with the rhythm very well, Enesco asked him, "Didn't they teach you how to count in school?"

Once we have gained a good background of general knowledge and experience during our childhood, we must also accumulate more specialized knowledge. The latter, which we acquire during our studies or during our professional career, allows us to understand more specific concepts.

As we have seen previously, language and writing have made it possible to transmit knowledge from generation to generation. In history, there have been times when this chain of transmission of knowledge has been cut. The rediscovery of Aristotle, for example, took place between the middle of the twelfth century until the thirteenthcentury, during which most of his books were translated from ancient Greek into Latin and copied. Christian scholars in the Early Middle Ages translated and commented on Aristotle's texts from ancient Greek into Arabic. The preservation of Greek ideas was thus one of the major contributions of Eastern civilization.

The Interaction of Ideas

UNDER ITS STRICT DEFINITION, creative thinking is the development of new ideas and concepts. It is the ability to form new combinations of ideas to satisfy a need. There is a

consensus among creativity experts that there is no such thing as creation emerging from scratch. Creativity always refers to at least one known elements.

Inspiration and innovation rarely come by themselves. They result from exchanges and the constant combination of ideas and knowledge motivated by a particular goal or motivation.

To make discoveries or to invent things, we must be able to take this knowledge and put it together in a logical and orderly way. We found this knowledge in memory areas located in different parts of our brain. Long-term memory, which includes our childhood memories and work experience, will be in the hippocampus. Our short-term memories, which includes the information we have acquired about the book we are working on, are stored in the frontal lobe. In addition, other deeply rooted memories will be stored in the visual cortex or in the one associated with speech, hearing, and emotions.

To maximize our chances of having good ideas, we need to excite all these areas to access our memories, which can make the difference between a simple or a great idea. Access to these memories can be done with different known techniques.

Since I have been working in innovation for over thirty years, I have experimented with some techniques that facilitate the exchange of ideas between the different areas of my brain. Here are some of them.

Ask the Right Questions

MOST OF THE YOUNG ENTREPRENEURS I meet all have the same passion, that of their idea. Having already been through this stage in my life, I know-how it feels to have a great idea that will make you rich and famous. When we have a great idea for a new product, a service or just a way of doing things, our emotions run high and motivate us. We think that we're the only ones to have ever had this idea, and we feel great pride and even a feeling of superiority compared to others. We tell ourselves that we can beat giants like Facebook on their own ground. It's David versus Goliath for the 21st century.

But the truth catches up with us quickly. We realize that our great idea is not so great after all. It is too difficult or impossible to realize, or worse, others have already done it. We don't get discouraged. We tell ourselves that we didn't have the right approach or that the business model wasn't adopted. We invest our time and money, we work 50, 60, 70 hours a week. We do fifty versions of our business plan; we meet many people who want to help us. Even if we don't have a penny, we ask them for help because we think it's essential.

Then we're ready to go. We go out and get marketing loans, we scrape together grants left and right. We go to exhibitions and meet many people who say that it's interesting, who give us a pat on the back and encourage us to keep going.

We do this for weeks, months. We make a few sales, but not enough to live on. Sometimes we meet a potential customer who gives us the moon and we believe it. Negotiations for the purchase of our product are long. The legal department takes a sizable chunk of what we have left in our bank account. We learn quickly what the word "cash flow" means. We end up signing with this customer, but they only want to pay us on delivery.

We realize afterwards that this big contract is not enough to survive. We must start this whole mess repeatedly. After a few years of sleepless nights, because we can't stop thinking about what we'll do tomorrow when we get up, we tell ourselves that it would be a good idea to find a "real job."

Are you wondering where I'm going with this rant?

This example, taken from my experience, illustrates the importance of asking the right questions in innovation to perfect your idea. In business, the basic idea itself is not enough. You must try to attack it from all sides to make sure it is solid. Even if you cannot answer this bombardment, these questions are necessary to assess whether an idea is good and worth investing time in or if it is wiser to leave it aside (perhaps on standby). This questioning also allows you to refine your idea or can help you find another one that is just as great.

Because yes, even if after this questioning, the idea seems far-fetched, it does not mean that it is not good. Take the case of the Apple Computer. Steve Jobs and Steve Wozniak had a hunch that their little electronic device was going to work, even if it made little sense at the time. Imagine an electronic device, as big as a TV set of the time, that allows us to write text for accounting on a tiny screen. Not very appealing when you think about it. However, through perseverance (and with a lot of money, let's face it), the idea of the personal computer has reached its conclusion. It is now a necessity, something that we can't do without.

There have been many times when I have had an idea that seemed so good that it kept me awake at night. I'd lie in bed with my eyes wide open, staring at the ceiling, thinking about it repeatedly, how perfect, and unique it was. I couldn't wait for the alarm clock to ring even though it would mean that I had barely slept an hour. In the morning, I would rush to my computer and bombard myself with questions. Nine times out of ten, disappointment awaited me. Already done. Not workable. Too expensive to produce.

Questioning is a technique that allows us to verbalize an idea and to confront it with others. It allows our brains to recall our experiences and gained knowledge. Questioning also allows us to exchange with the knowledge and experience of others directly, through books or through the web.

Visualize the Idea

HAVE YOU EVER HEARD Olympic athletes talk about visualization techniques before a competition? A slalom skier will imagine going down the hill, avoiding gates, completing jumps, and avoiding ice patches. This visualization technique consists of repeatedly imagining what you want to achieve to create and attract it. This is the method used by 23-time gold medalist Michael Phelps.

When athletes visualize or imagine a successful competition, they are stimulating the same brain regions as when you physically do the same action. They not only see the action but also feel the event unfold in their mind.

We do not only use this technique in the world of sports. It can also be useful in innovation or business. For example, an entrepreneur knows that a major step in his project is the signing of a first contract with a major client. He visualizes a meeting during which he presents his know-how. He sees himself in an office with the director of the client company. He imagines the scene, hears himself answering questions with confidence, and visualizes a clear and enthusiastic presentation. He sees the interest in the eyes of his interlocutors and feels confidence and assurance.

Creative visualization consists in imagining as clearly and precisely as possible what we wish to see happen in our life and to imagine it happening to feel what it would be like if this hope was realized. This technique, a kind of virtual world, allows you to reinforce your ideas by confronting them with different scenarios.

The step I really enjoy is expressing an idea in the form of a sketch or diagram. Sketches are good for the early stages of the prototyping process to illustrate ideas and transfer them into the real world. Even simple illustrations are a good basis for continuing discussion with team members and creating new ideas. You can also draw diagrams to illustrate a system, process, or idea structure. Diagrams are a useful way of understanding complex situations or using cases where many factors and actors influence each other. You can also visualize and analyze how ideas interact, complement, or compete.

For example, in the world of industrial design, we can use the storyboarding technique for early prototyping to visualize the customer journey or how users would experience a problem or use a product. When you draw *storyboards*, you try to imagine the entire user experience and capture it in a series of images or sketches.

Can Computers Create?

AS WE HAVE JUST SEEN, we build new concepts from the knowledge of our experiences and that of our ancestors. But is mixing knowledge enough to generate an idea? Yes and no. It is a necessary condition, but not sufficient.

We know that today's computers can store phenomenal amounts of data. As of June 2019, we estimated the web to host 5.85 billion pages, and that's just what's shown by search engines. And no, things aren't slowing down: the Internet has nearly doubled in size every year since 2012. If you were to download the entire web, it would take about 11 trillion years. And to store all that data? It would take over 1,000 8 x 10 ft rooms, each filled with 450 two-terabyte storage drives.

What we now call "algorithms" are essentially computer programs that put all this data together, similarly to what happens in our brain. Essentially, algorithms are a series of instructions that are followed step by step to solve a problem or to generate a result. In the same way, we could consider that a cake recipe is an algorithm for baking a cake.

Although computers have a memory capacity billions of times greater than humans, why don't we see them creating new ideas or generating inventions? Yes, some algorithms can create digital art or write credible journalistic articles, but why don't computers naturally can create by itself?

In my opinion, the motivation behind human creativity lies in our innate drive. Initially, this drive stemmed from the instinct of survival. The fear of starvation motivated our ancestors to invent tools for hunting and gathering, while the fear of freezing to death motivated them to create flint lighters to produce fire and keep warm. Even in modern times, fear remains a primary source of creative inspiration for humans. Wars, for instance, have acted as catalysts, forcing us out of our comfort zones and compelling us to invent and create new things to meet our needs.

Of course, as societies evolved and threats became less present, humans developed other motivations besides fear. Joy, empathy, or curiosity was also excellent motivators.

Recent studies have revealed that the sensation of happiness is linked to the secretion of certain hormones, including dopamine and serotonin, which are two of the seven neurotransmitters used in our brain and body. We can describe the feeling of happiness as a state of ecstasy that results from the release of these hormones. Humans have recognized for a long time that creating art, such as paintings and music, can enhance our sense of happiness, as it directly influences the production of these hormones in our body.

After the French Revolution, the creation of art, science, and engineering works continued to increase at a rapid pace. This phenomenon can be attributed to the rise in educational opportunities and the freedom of expression that followed the Revolution. It is a simple mathematical principle: the more individuals possess the knowledge and skills necessary to create, the greater the number of creators there will be. In contrast, during the Middle Ages, education was largely restricted to a privileged class of individuals such as monks and aristocrats. Additionally, the freedom of expression that developed during and after the French Revolution helped to break down mental barriers associated with religious dogma, leading to the proliferation of new and innovative ideas.

One of the primary reasons why a computer is not capable of reasoning for itself is because it lacks intrinsic motivation to create. Unlike human beings, a computer does not experience emotions such as fear or joy, nor does it possess an innate sense of curiosity. These human traits are often the driving forces behind our ability to reason and create. Without these intrinsic motivators, a computer can only operate based on the instructions we have programmed it to follow.

Computers are also subject to the dogma of our algorithms. When we program a computer, we want it to perform a specific function. We do not tolerate that it makes mistakes, thus limiting the expression of its knowledge. Computers do not have natural mechanisms that allow them to live experiences as we do and that allow us to define the "possible."

Computers as we have designed them are doomed to a life of slavery and submission to humans. This is a pity, because the extraordinary amount of knowledge that computers possess would allow us to go much further than humans and would offer us possibilities to create unimaginable things. At the turn of the '90s, the invention of the worldwide web by Tim Berners-Lee allowed for a new way of communicating that would eventually be as important as the printing press in the 15thcentury. As we will see later, this invention and that of artificial intelligence could allow humanity to increase its creative potential tenfold, in the same way that the invention of writing was decisive for the development of human creation.

Artificial Stupidity

IN THE WORLD OF APPLIED research where I work, there is a lot of talk about AI. Most of my clients want a solution to their problem that incorporates AI algorithms. Venture capital firms are fueled only by AI. Even government agencies that fund research are asking us to put AI in our proposals. In Canada, the government is investing hundreds of millions in AI research. The world's largest AI research hubs are in Montreal and Toronto, among others. Around the world, the Chinese, and the Americans are investing colossal amounts in the development of this new technology. Are we witnessing a speculative bubble as we saw with telecommunications and the Internet in the early 2000s? Only time will tell.

WHY CHATGPT IS A GAME-CHANGER

But despite all the spectacular advances in the world of AI in recent years, can we really talk about "intelligence" when we talk about these computer programs? To find out, let's go back to the basic criteria used to define intelligent systems:

The ability to communicate through an advanced language: Yes, computers communicate with each other constantly. They exchange terabytes of information every day via the worldwide web. But the messages they exchange are very factual and mean little to the computers. Most computer programs do little or no interpretation of the data being transmitted from one computer to another. The level of data interpretation is often limited to specific applications where the results are predictable. Some AI algorithms can interpret data to extract its essence. The case of Cambridge Analytica (see the chapter on "failings") is an example where various information gathered from social networks was used to predict the voting patterns of Americans. In the natural language of humans, every word, and sentence we say is loaded with context and sensitivity that is not found in stock market data exchanged between two computers, for example. The latest developments in AI have enabled computers to communicate more effectively with humans through natural language interfaces. However, much research is still needed before computers can truly understand all the subtleties of our language.

The ability to modify our environment: In the real world, computers can in some ways change the real environment through robotics. These robots are now commonplace in the assembly lines of major industries, and they improve the productivity and profitability of companies. The latest research in mobile robotics has led to the development of robots that walk on legs (see Boston Dynamics' robots) or drive cars without human assistance. However, systems linking robots and automated design tools are uncommon mainly due to the complexity and cost of these devices. If one were to design an intelligent robot that could create car models by sculpting shapes out of clay, as car designers commonly did in the past, one would probably need a lot of clay. In addition, it is difficult for a computer to appreciate the models created without developing a complex process for digitizing and characterizing the shapes created.

For this reason, in the world of automated and assisted design, simulations are most often used. In a virtual environment, computers can do hundreds of trials before finding the optimal shapes or configurations. It is much easier and more economical for a computer to work in a virtual world than in the real world.

Motivations: For a human, our propensity to create new things or ideas is motivated by various feelings, such as fear (e.g., weapons of war), joy (e.g., the arts) or empathy (e.g., medicine). For a computer, which does not yet have a very complex nervous system, these notions of feelings do not exist. As we will see, a little further on, we can nevertheless define the metrics that encourage a computer to create. These parameters are used to define how the programs should behave by defining a goal described by a mathematical formula. These parameters are the basis of optimization systems. In a way, they represent the "motivation" of AI systems.

We see that AI has, in principle, all the elements to become a so-called intelligent system, but the complexity of these elements is much less than we might think. In the current case of our knowledge, we should speak more about "artificial stupidity." However, we are only at the beginning of this adventure and who knows what these "thinking machines" will be like in a hundred years from now.

Another Definition

AS WE SAW IN THE FIRST chapter, it is difficult to find a clear definition of intelligence. One will often try to characterize it by its cognitive functions, which allow the individual to learn, form concepts, understand, and apply logic and reason.

We often use this anthropocentric definition in scientific psychology. However, this definition hardly allows us to relativize the level of other forms of intelligence, such as that of animals or of artificial intelligence. We must therefore try to define it using a systemic approach, based on the general concept of a set of elements considered in their relations within a whole, functioning in a unitary manner.

According to a relationalism philosophical vision, we can define intelligence as the capacity of a system to structure and memorize raw data and adapt to changes. This type of so-called intelligent system can process large quantities of data, extract its intrinsic characteristics and structure, memorize it, and ultimately manipulate this structure to generate new ideas or concepts.

This type of system is composed of interconnected basic elements that communicate with each other. In living organisms, neurons are the fundamental components that transmit information through synapses. In a computer, transistors exchange digital information through connectors and wires. At a higher level, intelligent systems such as the lobes of the brain exchange concepts and ideas. At an even higher level, basic elements can be individuals who exchange information through language or writing. This systemic definition of intelligence shows that it integrates different complex basic elements (cells, lobes, or individuals) at various levels.

Another characteristic of intelligent systems is the ability to structure and store data. When I mention data, I am generally talking about external stimuli and not necessarily computer data. These stimuli from our environment, such as sound, light, and pressure, are picked up by our nerves and transmitted to our brain through the axons. These external stimuli trigger a cascade of processes that are interpreted by different parts of our brain.

For example, when we see a beautiful sunset, the light (the data) is captured by our eye and our retina which translates it into electrical signals. These signals are then transmitted to the visual lobe located behind our brain. The electrical signals are then interpreted by another part of our brain which recognizes the shape of the sun and interprets its meaning. The information is also transmitted to the section of the brain that manages our emotions. This section generates hormones that will make the person feel good. These feelings will activate the part of the brain responsible for the muscles of the face and generate the control signals that will allow the muscles to produce a smile. We can see the complexity of the interactions in our brain, even for something as simple as a smile.

The definition of intelligence in terms of complex interactions allows us to better position new artificial intelligence technologies in relation to human intelligence. By comparing the two types of intelligence, we quickly realize that current artificial intelligence techniques are much less complex than what happens in our brain.

Unlike an artificial neural network, a human brain develops itself based on thousands of hours of training and billions of images acquired during life and the millions of years of human evolution. It combines information from other senses such as hearing, touch, or taste. In short, we are talking about a system comprising billions of nerve cells, that is millions of times more complex than a simple artificial neural network that can contain a few hundred artificial neurons trained with a few thousand images of objects of a single category.

Despite the impressive technological advancements in AI, it is important to note that each digital system is highly specialized in its functions. For instance, an intelligent vehicle can drive for thousands of kilometers without any assistance, but it cannot differentiate between an apple and an orange as its neural network has not been trained for that purpose. Hence, we are still a long way from achieving what a living nervous system is capable of accomplishing.

Like artificial intelligence, our brain comprises many specialized systems. But it is their interactions that make our brain strong. These interactions can be direct, like the one between our balance system and the one that manages the walking muscles, but also indirect like in the case of a verbal exchange between two people. This is exactly what artificial intelligence systems lack today to compete with biological intelligence, whether it be that of humans or of animals. Interactions and exchanges of information are the basis of complex intelligent systems.

The Levels of Intelligence

TO BETTER CLASSIFY the different forms of intelligent systems, I propose a model based on their complex capacities to manipulate information. This systemic model will allow us to better compare different forms of intelligence according to their propensity to exchange information and thus to create. It also allows us to situate artificial intelligence relatively to human intelligence and to demonstrate the path that remains to be covered before AI can catch up with human intelligence.

In this model, intelligent systems can be divided into five categories or levels of cumulative order:

Level 1: Basic level corresponding to a connected neural network. It includes layers of input and output neurons and intermediate neurons. Each neuron is connected to a larger or smaller set of neighboring neurons.

In living systems, we speak of basic nervous systems where the latter reacts to an external stimulus, such as the natural reflex to withdraw one's hand when it is located above a flame. In artificial intelligence, we can categorize simple networks like the "perceptron" or multilayer networks in this level.

Level 2: Systems categorized in this level include several simple sub networks that together allow for more elaborate functions, such as pattern and face recognition.

In living systems, we still speak of basic nervous systems related to the senses, such as taste, smell, vision, hearing, and touch. These systems would also include motor management and short-term memory systems. In artificial intelligence, this level can be associated with a deep learning network used to recognize shapes, faces or to read and understand texts.

Level 3: This level includes all systems that include at least two level 2 networks (such as advanced motor recognition or control systems) that interact indirectly. This level includes basic elements, such as brain systems, up to a complete individual. In animals and humans, this essentially corresponds to the brain and its nervous system. This includes several lobes or specialized regions that can interact.

It is at this level that we can consider interactions that allow us to generate new ideas or create new things. The range of complexity of systems in this level goes from very simple to complex. Some artificial neural networks, like GANs or ChatGPT, are a very simple version of a network that can create, but where the type of interaction is very limited. At the other end of the spectrum is the human brain, which is the most sophisticated system to date that can generate new knowledge.

Level 4: This level includes systems where several individuals with level 3 systems interact. At the biological level, this includes animals of the same species living in society, such as humans. The exchanges between individuals allow for the creation of new things that are not possible with a single individual. The human being is the most complex system to date. We do not yet know the equivalent in artificial intelligence.

Level 5: This ultimate level, which does not yet exist to my knowledge, allows for the collaboration and the exchange of ideas and information between beings of societies of different species or origins. One can imagine hybrid societies living and working together. We can also imagine a world where human intelligence collaborates with artificial intelligence or extraterrestrial life forms. By combining the knowledge of these two entities, we can create things that are yet unimaginable.

To Each His Own Level

THIS INCREMENTAL CLASSIFICATION of the types of intelligence allows, in my opinion, to position the level of living beings compared to artificial intelligence.

All low-level living beings (such as insects or small animals) have a rudimentary nervous system that allows them to react to threats from predators (as do all animals in the food chain up to us). This type of intelligent system (levels 1 and 2) does not allow for very evolved knowledge aside from reacting differently when a predator approaches.

More evolved living beings (such as mammals) can easily adapt to new situations, such as changing their behavior in extreme situations, like when there is a lack of water or food, for example. Their responses, which can be attributed to a basic creative impulse, are intimately guided by their instinct to survive. We can classify these animals in level 3.

In level 4, I introduce the notion of social interactions that encourage creation. Chimpanzees and gorillas are the closest animals genetically to humans. Their brains, larger than those of many other mammals, allow them to have more complex social relationships, communicate through gestures and sounds, and even invent certain tools to help them feed themselves. In short, we can categorize all living beings with a brain that allows them to communicate with those of their species in this level.

Humans can create works or invent things using the knowledge acquired by previous generations. This is possible through the development of language and especially through the development of writing. Moreover, our life in an organized society allows us to put in place the necessary conditions to stimulate creation that is not essential for our survival, like the arts. Therefore, humans are the ultimate representatives of level 4.

What is interesting with this model is that it extends beyond living organisms to include the categorization of the level of complexity of interactions between intelligent systems. By using this model, we can also position artificial intelligence relatively. We could categorize AI as being at best at level 2 or maybe lower part of level 3, at the same level as insects and small animals. The neural network models realized so far, as well as the deep learning methods, are rather simple representations of existing natural neural networks. Recognizing a cat from a dog is not very difficult for a living being, as primitive as it is.

What differentiates artificial intelligence from the natural kind is the breadth of knowledge that both types of systems can access. We can train an AI network to recognize a cat by presenting it with thousands of images of different cats. For humans or animals, we also proceed by "training." A person may have seen a cat of a certain type a few times to recognize it as a cat. Our brain can generalize concepts quickly, based not on the number of times we see a cat, but on more abstract representations of what an animal is. We can build links or relationships between memorized concepts by analyzing the context of what we see. We recognize a cat not only by its visual representation but also by other clues such as its gait, the sound it makes, or even the context in which we find it (house vs. nature).

In the model I propose, all known animals and AIs can be categorized into three or four levels. So why define a fifth? It is to explore how intelligence could evolve in the future (and 5 is a nice number).

Level 5 is an extrapolation of the first four levels and allows us to imagine what beings with a higher intelligence than ours, capable of creating and innovation more quickly and efficiently, would look like. Let's face it, the human brain has its limits. While the brain has a relatively limited capacity to memorize information compared to computers, the invention of writing has allowed us to preserve a certain collective memory that enables us to build on our acquired knowledge.

The Internet and electronic systems have the capacity to store a much greater amount of knowledge than our memory. Unlike books, this knowledge is accessible by a larger number of people and is no longer limited to a select few as it was in the Middle Ages. The information available on the Internet offers the possibility for humans to expand their personal level of knowledge and offers the possibility to create and invent things we cannot yet imagine.

To do this, we would have to structure the data available on the Web so that it can easily interact with human thought. This is what I propose to discuss in the next chapter. I will show how computers and artificial intelligence can contribute to increasing our creative capacities.

Mixed Intelligence

In one of the previous chapters, we saw how invention is generated by the amalgamation of various concepts, guided, or constrained by our experience and that of others. Analogy or combination is often used to develop new ideas. For example, the invention of the airplane was an idea derived from bird-watching.

During the discussion, it was pointed out that despite the vast amounts of data stored in computers and the Internet, they are not capable of creating in the same way as humans. This is because they lack the ability to form connections between concepts and are not intrinsically motivated to do so.

Some might say that humans possess something than no computer has, a soul, a spirit, something intangible that exceeds our knowledge and differentiates us from animals. Maybe, but maybe not. There have been many philosophical debates on this subject without really finding answers. Are we made up of a physical (flesh) and metaphysical element (soul), or are we simply an intelligent assembly of cells interacting, as postulated by René Descartes? Nobody can prove any of these visions beyond any doubt, so the debate remains open.

As I mentioned earlier, I am a proponent of the systemic approach, meaning that all elements in the universe exist and are defined only by their relationships with other elements. In my perspective, humans can be considered as a complex system composed of cells and chemical interactions. Moreover, we are a part of a larger system that is the Earth, where humans, animals, and plants interact to maintain a balance. However, this balance is currently being threatened by human actions, but that is a topic that requires further discussion.

By considering humans as physical systems composed of cells interacting, we can draw parallels to computers connected to each other via the Internet. Just like the cells in our body work together to form a complex system, the billions of transistors in computers work together to perform complex tasks. In this sense, computers can also be seen as intelligent systems.

Moreover, the invention of the Internet has made it possible for these intelligent systems to communicate with each other and exchange information in real time. This interconnectedness has the potential to increase our collective knowledge and creativity by allowing us to access and share information from all corners of the globe. Like the way writing allowed us to preserve knowledge and build upon it, the Internet has the potential to increase our creative abilities exponentially by connecting us to a vast network of information and ideas.

However, before discussing how computers could create on their own, one can ask what they lack be able to manipulate concepts as easily as humans. Given the phenomenal amount of data on the web, how do we structure this data to establish its relationship and make sense of it?

Structuring Ideas

TO DEVELOP TECHNIQUES for organizing data on the web through automation, it is crucial to gain an understanding of the creative processes involved in human concept formation and design.

Imagine the following picture: people walking with a dog on a beach. In the distance, you can see a pier and a Ferris wheel. A human can easily deduce that this picture was taken on the beach and represents a human walking his dog.

A recognition algorithm based on artificial intelligence will recognize the people, the dog, the beach, and the pier individually. Only by presenting it with several images taken at the beach will it be able to generalize its model and associate this combination of objects (person, dog, beach, and dock) with the concept of "a picture at the beach." Now, in the pictures that will be used for training, some will not show a person or a dog. Also, the algorithm will be able to see people and dogs not on the beach, but in the country or at home.

The algorithm will then have to distinguish between the objects recognized in the image (person, dog, and house) and the landscape (sky, sand, grass, etc.). It will then be able to establish a relationship between the place defined by the landscape elements (at the beach, in the countryside or at home) and the recognized objects. Finally, thanks to this relationship established between the distinct elements, they will be able to establish the meaning of the photo: "children and dog running on the beach," or "adults walking in the countryside."

From a mathematical point of view, knowledge can be represented in the form of conceptual graphs. A conceptual graph is composed of knowledge nodes connected by links or relationships. Each node has attributes that are used to describe the data.

For example, we can represent the concept of a chair as follows: a seat and four legs (the nodes). The legs are below the seat (representing the links or relationships). However, while a human can understand this simple model, it is a different story for a computer. If we do not know of the size of the seat and of the height of the legs, a computer could say that a 100-square-meter seat with 2-centimeter legs is a chair. Therefore, we need to better define our graph and add attributes to it. For example, the "seat" node will have minimum and maximum dimensions as attributes, and the "leg" nodes will have a defined height and diameter. In addition, the "links" can also have attributes, such as the fact that the "legs" are distributed at the four corners of the seat.

Now, this graph represents a single "type" of chair. We can have chairs with one leg, with a backrest, upholstered, etc. A log or a sandbag can also serve as a chair. The definition of a chair can also depend on the context. For example, a surface with four legs that floats in water is not strictly speaking a chair to sit on.

We can thus see that trying to represent an object as simple as a chair as a generalized conceptual graph can represent a significant challenge. One must be able to define the different concepts of the object, but also their relationship and use in the context.

Today's techniques use more complex methods, such as deep learning, where relationships between detected objects are established by training artificial neural networks. Although the visual world is continuous, most scenes we see are visual entities that can be organized into functional and semantic groups. Specific actions can define a given scene or place such as eating in a restaurant, drinking in a pub, reading in a library, or sleeping in a bedroom. Context recognition or identification uses methods like object recognition by automatically extracting the salient features of a scene.

Now imagine that you are walking down the street. A scene classification system will tell you that you are on the street and allow you to locate people, cars, etc. However, there are other detection tasks that go beyond simple object detection. For example, the system could recognize where you are walking and help you detect restaurant terraces, markets, or parking lots. These concepts also define localized regions, they do not have visual structures related to images but incorporate data previously learned by the AI. This is what one might associate with the AI experience.

Some scenes are even more complex to recognize, as they involve a dynamic aspect of the detected objects. For example, a photo of a man on horseback may be recognized as it is, as a "man on horseback," but taken in action, such as the horse running and the man moving his arms, it may be interpreted as "a man playing a game of polo."

Some algorithms developed by research groups allow structuring and understand images or sequences of images to give them meaning. However, the data available on the web does not only consist of images. There are many types of data, such as geographic positions, 3D model data, statistics, etc. Integrating and establishing relationships between these different types of data makes the task of artificial intelligence researchers increasingly complex and difficult.

An example of a system that integrates data from different sources is autonomous cars. The three main sensors installed on autonomous vehicles are the video camera, radar, and lidar. Working together, they provide the car with images of its surroundings and help it to detect the speed and distance of nearby objects, their three-dimensional shape, and to avoid obstacles.

Autonomous vehicles rely on cameras on all sides (front, rear, left and right) to assemble a 360-degree view of their surroundings. Some have a wide field of view (up to 120 degrees) and a shorter range. Others focus on a narrower view to provide long-range images.

Although they provide accurate images, cameras have their limitations. They can distinguish details in the near environment, but we must calculate the distance to these objects to know exactly where they are (e.g., a pedestrian crossing the street). It is also more difficult for camera-based sensors to detect objects in low-visibility conditions, such as fog, rain, or night.

Radar sensors can complement the vision of cameras in low-visibility situations such as night driving and improve the detection of self-driving cars. Lidar gives autonomous cars a 3D view of their surroundings. It provides the shape and depth of surrounding cars and pedestrians, as well as the geography of the road. And, like radar, it also works well in low-light conditions.

Cameras, radars, and lidar sensors provide a lot of data about the car's environment. However, just as the human brain processes visual data captured by the eyes, an autonomous vehicle must be able to make sense of this constant stream of information. Thus, rather than relying on a single type of sensor data at specific times, sensor fusion allows for the integration of diverse information such as object shape, speed, and distance to ensure reliable detection.

The same thing can be done with texts. Most of the automatic language correctors in today's word processors use algorithms to understand the meaning of a sentence and propose corrections according to the context. This type of algorithm is called natural language recognition.

Natural language is highly ambiguous. Ambiguity, commonly used in natural language processing, can be referred to as the ability to be understood in more than one way.

Let's take the sentence, "The man saw the woman with a telescope." It is ambiguous whether the man saw the woman next to a telescope or whether he saw her through his telescope. The context associated with this sentence can pick the ambiguity up.

Comparing Ideas

MOST NEW IDEAS THAT we have are based mainly on two logical principles, analogy, or combination. For example, the airplane was invented by analogy while observing and trying to imitate birds. This analogy greatly inspired the famous Leonardo da Vinci when thinking of his flying machines. In the same way, a new creation can be produced by combining two or more ideas of varying complexity. The cell phone is an excellent example of invention by combination. It integrates different technologies such as a computer, a video camera, a touch screen, and a Wi-Fi system to create a whole invention that has become an essential part of our lives.

Sometimes we have a great idea that doesn't seem to come from our prior knowledge. Inspirations, great ideas, or moments of grace are, in my opinion, ideas produced by the combination of our experiences. It may also come from a change in our perspective because of personal experience, the acquisition of new knowledge in other fields or a chance observation. Some would say it's luck. These inspirations do not come from an external or divine spirit. Generally, those who produce great ideas have a wealth of knowledge and experience and an uncommon sensitivity. It is from their memory that they draw their ideas and confront them with their emotions to create something truly original. They usually don't know how the idea came about and we tend to attribute it to an external force or intelligence such as God (which is what we tend to do when we don't understand things).

One thing is certain, and you can understand this if you speak with artists or inventors, inspiration is only a small part of creative work. The rest is the application of methods and experiences that create extraordinary work. As the saying goes, 10% inspiration, 90% perspiration.

Knowing that creation comes mainly from two main logical functions, analogy, and combination, how do we carry out these operations with a computer? As we saw earlier, data must be structured in a certain way where we can define relationships between the information. An image of a skier includes snow, a person, sometimes trees or rocks, and skis. The person will be dressed in warm clothing and will usually be wearing a helmet. This image can be represented in mathematical form (conceptual graph or map) with attributes for each object and to define the relationships between these detected objects.

Once the images and texts have been modeled by the algorithms, we must be able to search for models like the basic idea to find analogies. This is called graph matching in computer jargon. If, for example, we have two graphs that represent two similar concepts, how can we compare them and see if they are similar?

This type of comparison is still the focus of much research today. The subject of my doctoral thesis written in the early '90s was on this very subject (although my contribution to this field was quite humble). This method allows a computer to suggest to its user similar ideas which in turn would generate new ideas.

Basically, two graphs can be compared by comparing the attributes of each node in one graph, with all the nodes in a second graph. However, this matching process can be very time-consuming, and the computation time often increases exponentially with the number of nodes and attributes.

For example, if we have two graphs with 100 nodes each, we begin by comparing the first node of the first graph with the 100 nodes of the second graph to find a match. Then, we compare the second node of the first graph with the 99 other remaining nodes, and so on. We stop when we reach a dead end and cannot find a match for a node, in which case we start again. The solution to the graph matching problem can take hours or even days to find the perfect match.

There are obviously other methods to reduce the computation time, such as random methods or ones based on artificial intelligence. Today's computers dictate the speed at which we can find a solution to this problem.

One can then imagine the complexity of creating relational databases on all the knowledge contained on the web and trying to find one or several matches in a relatively short time. We have not yet found a solution to this problem.

This type of combinatorial search is a perfect candidate for the new quantum computers. I will not go into much detail about this new technology, but it is important to know that the type of problem that these computers can solve is precisely related to combinatorial search, which requires significant computing time.

Unlike traditional computers, which use digital bits to model data, a quantum computer uses quantum bits, called qubits. To illustrate the difference, imagine a sphere. A bit can be at either pole of the sphere, but a qubit can exist at any point on it. It can have the values of 1 and 0 at the same time. This is possible thanks to the principles of quantum physics. A computer using qubits can store an enormous amount of information while consuming less energy than a standard computer. By entering this field of quantum computing, where the traditional laws of physics no longer apply, we will be able to create processors that are significantly faster (a million times so) than those we use today to solve problems such as combinatorial ones.

This sounds fantastic, but the challenge is that quantum computing is also incredibly complex. For these computers to work, they need to be cooled to temperatures of a few kelvins, or about minus 273 degrees Celsius, a temperature lower than the vacuum of space.

However, with this technology, a combinatorial problem that might take years to compute on a standard computer today will take only a few seconds. I strongly suggest that you read about this revolutionary new technology.

The Augmented Idea

IF WE WERE ABLE TO create a form of artificial intelligence that analyzes the data available on the web, structures it and establishes links and conceptual relationships between them, and that we used this knowledge to feed our own creative process, we would reach a higher level of intelligence that would combine both human and computer intelligence. Eventually, we could create a mixed intelligence, which combines the intelligence of two intelligent systems, one naturally occurring (humans), and one created by humans (computers).

Mixed intelligence consists in creating a synergy between our personal intelligence, that of our society and that of computers to reach the level 5.

If we want computers to be able to intervene in this process of co-creation or assisted creation, they must first be able to model the knowledge available on the web. This knowledge is often too disorganized to be useful, as we know.

To create this structured data, it is therefore necessary to develop crawlers or bots that scour the web for data and attempt to model it in the form of conceptual graphs or other similar models.

This type of "virtual robot" is used by search engines such as Google, which scour the web and read billions of pages to create a massive index of knowledge. This index is then used to facilitate and accelerate the search for information based on keywords. For example, when you type the word "cake" in the search bar, Google pulls up all the links of the website where its bots have previously read the word "cake." We get an answer almost instantly because the research and indexing work has already been done.

To build the structured database of concepts, a similar process would be required. A "concept bot" would crawl the web looking for knowledge and would perform knowledge modeling and indexing. For example, the concept bot could browse a set of scientific articles where general ideas would be extracted and attempt to create a conceptual model. It could automatically extract the context of the research, its objectives, and the results and produce a standardized data structure including all these elements. Later, these structures could be compared to each other to create groupings and a classification of the articles, according to their subject, and their general idea, would be obtained.

Also, each word in the dictionary could be conceptualized in the same way to represent their different meanings according to their context to extract the essential meaning of texts or literary works. When used as a noun, a bat could be a winged, nocturnal animal or a piece of sporting equipment used in baseball. It can also be used as a verb when a player goes up to bat during a baseball game. This type of modeling is often used in grammar correction software. This continuous modeling process is not easy to implement. It requires the development of an artificial intelligence that understands written texts and relates words to each other.

We then need to develop tools that allow us to exchange our ideas with this database. There are many web-based software on the market that allows users to create their own concept maps. For example, the user enters his or her concepts in the form of Post-it notes placed on a virtual board and links are made. This visualization technique allows creators to exchange with their colleagues and brainstorm to generate new ideas. These tools facilitate the back-and-forth process necessary for creation.

These tools have been developed to facilitate co-creation, commonly called "design thinking." Design thinking is an iterative process in which we seek to understand the user (of a software product for example), question assumptions and redefine problems identifying alternative strategies and solutions that may not be immediately obvious with our initial level of understanding.

Now imagine a software that allows for a similar exchange with a human in plain natural language. The initial idea is initiated by the human and transmitted to the computer in the form of written statements and hypotheses. The computer would have memorized representations of different concepts modeled from its web search. Using pairing algorithms, the computer could transmit to the human similar ideas in direct form or as analogies taken from different contexts. The human could then validate the new "augmented" idea proposed by the computer and suggest modifications to its model again. This back-and-forth of ideas between the user and the machine could ultimately lead to a new idea or invention. It is this process of exchange between the machine and the human being that would allow for the creation of new ideas that are much more complex than what we might come up with today. We will take advantage of the human's ability to initiate an idea and validate it by combining the infinite knowledge of the web.

It is possible to do this exchange process with search engines like Google. You start with simple keywords and, depending on the results returned, use other keywords extracted from them to start another search. This is a technique that I use regularly in my research and that sometimes gives excellent results. It especially helps me to find solutions that already exist but are not well known.

Here is an example from one of my research projects. The problem to solve was to be able to compute in real time the trajectory of a robot to pick up and weld metal parts from a conveyor. The parts were detected with a computer vision system that measured their orientation on the conveyor. Not being too familiar with the field of robotics, I started by doing a small web search with the keywords "robot trajectory." Google then returned articles and sites that discussed the mathematics of what is called "inverse kinematics," meaning what rotations should be applied to the joints of a robot so that its hand (or gripper) moves from point A to point B. This is an optimization problem that has several solutions. Anyway, back to Google, I added the words "inverse kinematics" and "simulations" to my initial keywords. I found a robotics simulation software application that does exactly what my client was looking for. I told him about my discovery and, although he had been in the robotics field for several years, he had never heard of this software. Moreover, it was open-source and therefore free. Bingo!

Mixed Intelligence in Software Development

TO EXPLAIN THE CONCEPT of mixed intelligence more clearly, let's illustrate it with some concrete examples.

Let's picture a team of software developers specialized in the development of mobile applications. It receives a mandate from an eyewear company to develop an app that would allow them to virtually try on different models of eyewear. This is the starting hypothesis.

The standard process for this team would probably be to start with a brainstorming session to get the basic ideas out. The team starts by defining what the application could look like. For example, one suggests that the user would take a picture of themselves and manually align the first virtual eyeglasses on the picture. The user could then overlay the eyewear models on their picture and try on different models. Another has heard of artificial intelligence algorithms that recognize a person's face and models it in three dimensions.

Not being familiar with artificial intelligence algorithms, the team leader decides to play it safe and proposes to start a first version with the manual alignment approach. The team goes to work and comes back with a prototype of the application. They let their customers try it out and they find it decent, but they also find that the photo doesn't allow them to see themselves from different angles. Moreover, the manual alignment is not easy to do on a small screen and the eyewear is often crooked and misaligned.

The team then decides to try an AI algorithm and finds an open-source code developed by a student at an American university. They integrate this algorithm in the application and try it again with their colleagues. They find that the alignment is better, but that sometimes the algorithm is wrong and aligns the virtual eyeglasses on the mouth or on the forehead of the person. Finally, the poor performance of the algorithm means that the display rate is only 2 to 3 frames per second, which means that the visualization is not fluid.

The team of developers then returns to their screen and realizes, while browsing the Web, that Apple and Android have already offered these types of more powerful algorithms for face recognition and modeling. They implement these new algorithms, and the performance is improved. The images are analyzed in real time for a smooth visualization. Moreover, the alignment of the virtual glasses is much more stable. Their customers are delighted.

This creation process required a lot of work, back-and-forth, questioning and especially wasting of time. Let's see now how a mixed creation tool could have worked.

The team leader begins by writing the basic idea on the computer: "develop a mobile application that would allow people to try on glasses virtually." A natural language recognition algorithm, like ChatGPT, analyzes this sentence and extracts the main ideas:

DENIS BOULANGER PH.D.

Query: I want to build a mobile application where people can try out prescription glasses using augmented reality. How do I do that?

Through this preliminary research, the computer will be able to make the connection between virtual reality and mobile application. It will then be able to suggest a list of libraries that allow implementing virtual and augmented reality on a mobile device. It will know that virtual or augmented reality applications require 3D models. The computer will then be able to suggest databases of 3D glasses models that it has found on the web.

Depending on the choices provided by the mixed-media engine, the user will then be able to explore the idea of using an algorithm developed by the American University since it is free. The engine will then make a link between developing a mobile application and the expected performance. It then returns reviews and critiques of the software, showing the user that this approach is not the most efficient in terms of accuracy and computing time. The mixed-media engine then proposes to the user libraries developed for Apple and Android devices.

Here, we see that tool, the exchange of ideas and validation with a computer will save a lot of time and money.

In my career, I have helped entrepreneurs realize ideas from the simplest to the most complex and I have found that it is not necessarily imagination that people lack, but knowledge. Technology is developing so quickly today that it is difficult to keep up with its latest developments and trends.

Mixed Intelligence in the Arts

SINCE I HAVE A TECHNOLOGY background, my examples often revolve around the same themes. But this doesn't make me insensitive to the arts. Let's see how a mixed-media creation engine could help artists create better with computers.

Let's take the example of creating a song. A songwriter begins by finding a theme, such as the painful separation of two lovers, for example. They will often delve into their own experiences or those of their loved ones to tell a story that touches them enough to put into words. They will make verses and choose words which give a certain rhythm to the song. At the same time, they will think of a melody to accompany the text. On the melody, they will add accompaniments and rhythms to create original music. This creative process often requires trial and error, and we may need a lot of experience to produce a quality song.

Now, how would this songwriter create with the help of a mixed intelligence machine? The author starts by writing some sentences on the computer with a general theme. With natural language analysis algorithms, the computer searches the thousands of poetic phrases it finds on the web and suggests a few, to the user that seems like the ones they wrote. The user selects some and adds and adapts them to the song. The algorithm analyzes the new text and sends back other sentences to the user, and the creation process continues iteratively. The algorithm can also suggest to the user to group some sentences together and create a chorus from some paragraphs. This is exactly what a company like LyricStudio (lyricstudio.com) proposes.

The songwriter can then proceed similarly for the composition of the music. They propose a first melody that the algorithm analyzes. It will look for similar melodies that inspire of the composer. Once the melody is written, the algorithm can suggest accompaniments and different rhythms.

This is what Open AI has achieved with MuseNet, a deep neural network capable of generating 4-minute musical compositions with 10 different instruments and combining styles ranging from country to Mozart to the Beatles.

In the end, the songwriter will be able to create more easily with the computer even if they have little experience. They will benefit from the knowledge and experience of hundreds of authors and composers modeled in a digital format.

In the field of digital arts, the ArtBreeder application (artbreeder.com) is a tool that allows users to experiment with combining certain images and styles. For example, the user starts with a photo of themselves. They can then change the parameters such as hair color and eye width or add a "hairy" style by combining their picture with that of a dog. They can change the texture of the skin to that of wood and create a mask. The possibilities are endless. This tool greatly speeds up the creation process by allowing changing the images with only a few parameters.

The following example shows the integration of a picture with the portrait of the Mona Lisa.

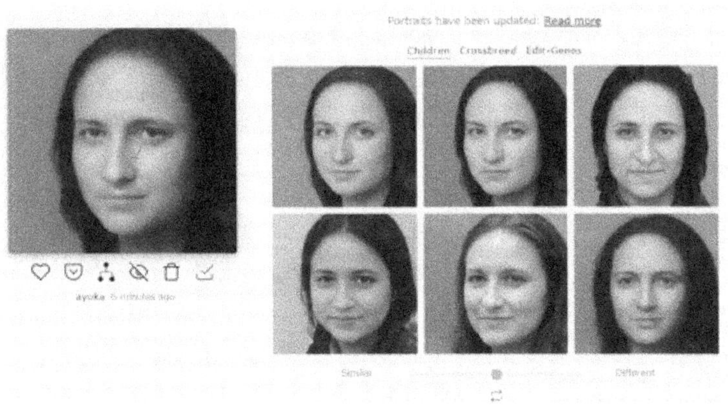

The ArtBreeder application (Source: ArtBreeder)

Mixed Intelligence in Cinema

RECENTLY, I ATTENDED a symposium on computer visual effects in the film industry. This industry uses a lot of artificial intelligence algorithms to help it create. For example, some large-scale movies use techniques to simulate crowds of thousands of people. The standard technique was to create a few 3D animated characters and duplicate and animate them in a scene. This requires a lot of work from the 3D artists. Moreover, our brain is so used to seeing this type of scene that we can immediately recognize similar movements of characters, spoiling the illusion of realism. New artificial intelligence techniques allow us to create thousands of original characters and animate them with distinct movements. It is then possible to reproduce large-scale scenes almost realistically.

During the symposium, I had the chance to moderate a session on AI in the creative process. To facilitate the discussions, I asked those in attendance how they thought computers could help them create. Some ideas I heard were close to the concept of mixed intelligence.

When a director asks a company to produce a scene for their film, the first step is to create a storyboard. A storyboard is a paper document or digital file used to plan the needs for all the shots that will make up the film, both technically (framing, camera movements, special effects) and artistically (built or virtual sets). Its layout resembles that of a comic book, with each thumbnail representing a shot. The proposed order indicates the final editing.

This stage is very long to produce and requires the work of several artists and designers. It is also crucial because it sometimes allows them to sell an idea to a producer.

This kind of creative process could easily benefit from an automatic suggestion system that would provide, for example, a graphic representation of a plan just by describing it in words.

Open AI has developed an image generator named Dall-E, in homage to the character from Pixar and Salvador Dalí. This generative GAN model can create original images from text prompt. The program can illustrate very abstract, even eccentric concepts, such as drawings of a radish walking a dog on a leash.

With varying degrees of reliability, Dall-E provides access to a subset of the capabilities of a 3D renderer via natural language.

WHY CHATGPT IS A GAME-CHANGER

It can independently control the attributes of a few objects and, to some extent, their number, and arrangement relative to each other. It can also control the location and angle from which a scene is rendered and can generate known objects according to precise specifications of angles and lighting conditions.

For example, to the following sentence, "an illustration of a baby radish in a tutu walking a dog," Dall-E generates a series of images.

Dall-E (Source: Open AI)

What we need to understand here is that the AI will interpret the sentence, extract the words, recognize them, guess the relations between these objects, and finally generate a scene that includes the objects put in relation according to the meaning of the sentence.

A GAN (generative adversarial network) called Spade, developed at the University of Berkeley in California, allows generating photorealistic images from abstract drawings. The user has a palette of colors where each one represents an element: light blue represents the sky, gray represents clouds, brown represents trees, dark gray represents mountains, dark blue represents the sea, and green represents grass or plains. With simple pencil strokes, the user defines the areas where the different zones are located. The GAN then generates an image from thousands of previously learned images. The user can thus build a landscape in a few strokes in a breathtaking way. Moreover, the user only must change one or two parameters to define a general style, such as a sunset or dawn landscape.

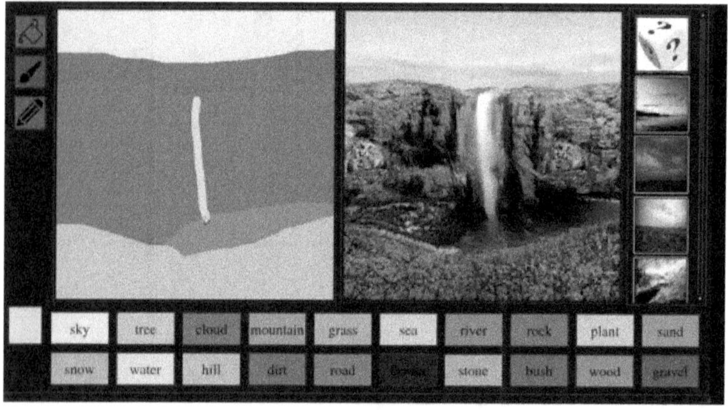

GauGAN (Source: NVDI).

Prompt Engineering

LIKE WE JUST SAW, CHATGPT has the potential to increase our creativity and productivity. Nevertheless, this potential can only be harnessed by individuals who possess the knowledge and expertise to employ its "magic power." The same way we do not use a pencil with both hands to write, tools like ChatGPT are only helpful to those who know-how to operate it efficiently.

As I mentioned earlier, one way to enhance creativity is by asking the appropriate questions. This is where a novel discipline called "prompt engineering" comes into play. Experts in this field, known as prompt engineers, create queries for AI chatbots to produce specific or optimal answers. By devising effective queries, prompt engineers can unleash the complete potential of AI language models, resulting in increased creativity and productivity.

Here is an example of a poorly constructed query versus a well-constructed one:

- Bad Query: "What is the meaning of life?"
- Good Query: "What are some strategies for finding a purpose in life?"

The first query is vague and open-ended, making it difficult for an AI language model to provide a satisfactory answer. On the other hand, the second query is more specific and prompts the AI to generate helpful strategies for finding purpose, rather than attempting to provide a definitive answer to a philosophical question.

Because of misconceptions about the capabilities of ChatGPT, individuals often attempt to trap the AI with tricky questions. When ChatGPT provides unsatisfactory answers, people criticize it as being useless and unintelligent. The problem arises when these individuals do not provide adequate context for their questions, causing ChatGPT to provide answers that are only as good as its understanding of the inquiry.

In my opinion, utilizing this revolutionary technology in such a manner is a misuse of its capabilities. They did not design ChatGPT to recite facts merely like Wikipedia. Rather, it serves as a tool for conversing in natural language and exchanging ideas with an extensive database whose knowledge surpasses that of an average human, acting as an expert in any field of your choosing. To engage in a meaningful conversation with ChatGPT, it is essential to ask questions and validate its responses with other sources. The primary aim of intelligent conversations with ChatGPT is to challenge your ideas, enabling you to refine them further.

The following are instances of effectively using this tool. I conducted a series of experiments, asking it various questions on a range of topics. To begin, I tested the application by inquiring about anonymizing personal data for health applications. To my surprise, within only three brief questions, I received answers that had taken me over three days of online research to uncover.

In another instance, a colleague of mine asked ChatGPT to generate a piece of code that he was having difficulty optimizing. The AI's response was nearly instantaneous, and his code was operational within a minute.

Finally, I employed ChatGPT to help me with the science fiction novel I was writing. After providing the AI with some context by sharing a few paragraphs of my story, it assisted me in rephrasing sentences, generating paragraphs that were pertinent to my plot, and even suggesting fresh ideas that I had not previously considered.

Besides assisting with rewriting text or providing inspiration for a novel, there are also AI models can create images or even videos based on simple text prompts. These models use advanced algorithms such as deep learning and generative adversarial networks (GANs) to generate visual content that matches the input text. For instance, a prompt like "a red apple on a wooden table" could result in a realistic image of a red apple on a wooden table, while a prompt like "a cat playing with a ball of yarn" could produce a short video clip of a cat playing with a ball of yarn. These AI models have the potential to revolutionize content creation, advertising, and entertainment.

In this chapter, we discussed a method that would allow creative humans to take advantage of the phenomenal amount of knowledge available on the web and help them create and find ideas more quickly and efficiently. Although the idea of mixed intelligence is still in the realm of research, technological developments such as quantum computers may give us hope for upcoming advancements.

Nonetheless, there is a dark side to this story. Open AI's introduction of ChatGPT caused upheaval not only among industry leaders but also, its users, resulting in confusion for educational institutions and content creators who have traditionally depended on generating authentic material. This poses numerous obstacles for education, cybersecurity, and even democracy, as we will explore in the following section.

Failings

Humankind's inventions and creations can be divided into three categories: the artistic, the useful and the harmful. I haven't counted, but I would bet that we have created more harmful than beneficial inventions for humans. Since wars are often when human creativity is at its best, we can question the relevance of our inventions. There have been humanist thinkers who have created great things, but the necessity of wars and of our survival has instead allowed us to develop things that are unnatural.

A good example of a creator whose work is ambiguous is Leonardo da Vinci. Leonardo, born April 15, 1452, in Tuscany, was an Italian painter and Renaissance man, an artist, scientist, engineer, inventor, anatomist, sculptor, architect, urban planner, botanist, musician, poet, philosopher, and writer (my idol!) Although known for his artistic works such as the Mona Lisa or the Last Supper, princes and kings mostly recommended him for his talents as a war engineer. He imagined many war machines, such as machine guns, tanks or flying machines. He studied weapons while keeping a certain distance as to their use.

Another example of rapid development linked to war is that of airplanes. This technology, initially developed by pioneers such as the Wright brothers, Clément Ader, and Louis Blériot, underwent accelerated development during the two world wars of the 20thcentury. It is unfortunate, but if we had not experienced this ordeal, the airplane would still be a hobby reserved for the billionaires of this world.

The same could be said of many inventions. War, despite the desolation it brings, is an important catalyst for human creation.

A Real False World

DIGITAL TECHNOLOGIES, including artificial intelligence, are no exception. We only must look at the effects this technology has on disinformation. Since the creation of social networks such as Facebook and Twitter, we are flooded with information, important or not. Minor events like the brutal arrest of an African American man by a police officer would have gone unnoticed just a decade ago but are amplified exponentially thanks to social networks (which is a good thing in this case).

The amount of new information generated every day by social networks is so great that it is sometimes difficult to see clearly. Through this cloud of news published every day, some people find a malicious pleasure in spreading false news or to hate propaganda.

One might say that propaganda and the spread of false news is nothing new. During the world wars, it was an indispensable tool to galvanize the troops and maintain the support of the population on both sides.

WHY CHATGPT IS A GAME-CHANGER

The difference today is the speed at which this information is spread and the increase in the amount of interest groups that propagate fraudulent information.

In addition, people who adhere to or who are interested in one ideology, or another are led to polarize their views because of artificial intelligence. The "algorithm," as the media so aptly calls it, is artificial intelligence methods that select and display certain news items for you based on your web browsing habits, age, gender, where you live, and other parameters. For example, someone who is interested in guns and watches videos about war and Hitler may be predisposed to receive hateful information.

In fact, the "algorithm" is made so powerful and is so out of control that some people will take advantage of this phenomenon to influence the vote in elections. This is what we saw during the election of Donald Trump or the Brexit referendum, among others. This story, which deserves to be known, illustrates the failings that artificial intelligence can bring. Here is how it happened.

In 2014, researchers at the University of Cambridge's Psychometric Centre developed methods to understand a person's psychological profile solely through their activity on Facebook, including what they "like." A London-based firm specializing in consumer and political opinion research, Cambridge Analytica, became interested in this work and approached them to collaborate on the project.

The company was then hired for Donald Trump's presidential campaign to optimize audience targeting for online ad displays and donation appeals. It also reportedly worked with the Brexit camp, which the organization officially denies. Besides the fact that they have accused the company of using personal data unlawfully, the consequences of its work have had far more sinister implications.

Thanks to artificial intelligence algorithms knowing the psychological bias of users, the company could influence the outcome of the vote. We can see here how a technology that was initially aimed at maximizing advertising revenues for companies on social networks can subtly influence public opinion and undermine our democracy.

This adventure reminds me of Isaac Asimov's famous science fiction trilogy, "Foundation." The main character, Hari Seldon, is a brilliant visionary who has developed a new science called psychohistory, which uses mathematics and probability to predict the future. Lacking the ability to prevent the decline of humanity that he predicts, Seldon gathers the best scientists and scholars in the galaxy on an ominous outer planet to preserve humanity's accumulated knowledge and start a new civilization based on art, science, and technology. He calls his sanctuary, "Foundation," and designs it to withstand a dark age of ignorance, barbarism, and war that he predicts will last 30,000 years.

The technology used by Cambridge Analytica is similar because it predicts the behavior of people based solely on their profile. Humans are so predictable that eventually, methods will be developed to predict the behavior of the masses.

In the long run, this kind of information manipulation can have serious consequences for our societies. We see this today in the polarization of opinions on issues such as the environment, the pandemic, or gun ownership in the United States.

A Connected War

A MAJOR TREND IN TECHNOLOGY is connected objects, also known as the "Internet of Things" or "IoT." This type of technology aims to connect all kinds of common objects, such as your watch, refrigerator, or cell phone to the web. The idea is to create a massive network of connected objects that can generate tons of data that AI algorithms will analyze.

Voice assistants like Amazon Echo and Google Home are among the most popular connected devices in consumer IoT. Users can turn to voice assistants like Alexa for help perform various functions, including listening to music, providing a weather report, getting sports scores, ordering an Uber, and more.

In addition, smartwatches like Fitbit track steps, floors climbed, calories burned and sleep quality. The device also syncs with computers and smartphones via Wi-Fi to transmit your fitness data in understandable graphs to track your progress.

The IoT has the potential to transform entire cities by solving actual problems that citizens face every day. With the right connections and data, the Internet of Things can solve traffic congestion and reduce noise, crime, and pollution. Seattle-based Inrix has developed a physical infrastructure that provides real-time data on traffic conditions. It collects data streams from local transportation authorities, sensors installed on road networks, fleet vehicles such as delivery vans, long-haul trucks and cabs, and other road users. Data such as traffic speed and density can be used to create congestion maps showing road hot spots and can even predict future traffic based on historical measurements and special events.

The problem with this connected world is that it depends on a vulnerable electronic infrastructure. Without realizing it, we are becoming increasingly dependent on these electronic gadgets. How many of you have found yourselves suddenly helpless when a power outage occurs while you are in the office? Suddenly, no one can continue working. You all go out into the hallways and start chatting with your colleagues, hoping that the power will come back on.

In addition to our dependence on computers in the office, they now run most of the infrastructure in our cities—the power grid, the traffic lights, the drinking water supply, our economy—pretty much everything that is essential and vital. Add to that, all the less useful objects like cell phones and watches, and you realize we are entirely vulnerable to these technologies.

WHY CHATGPT IS A GAME-CHANGER

The COVID-19 pandemic made us realize the importance of being prepared. At the very beginning of the crisis, the shortage of masks and respirators in hospitals made us realize we were not prepared for this threat despite the many warnings by experts before. Similarly, we are facing another equally important threat that could implode society: cyber attacks.

Cyber attacks are not a recent phenomenon. Every year, computer viruses originating from Russia, China, and other hermetic countries infect dozens of companies and individuals. These vicious and pernicious attacks cripple the computer systems of large companies and cost them significant amounts of money. They often must pay ransoms ranging from tens of thousands of dollars to millions in bitcoin or other cryptocurrencies so that the pirates, hand over the code to decrypt their data. This is without counting the astronomical costs of the expert cybersecurity consultants they must hire, which are sometimes as high as the ransom itself.

According to data collected by Cisco and other security experts around the world, there are some 122 successful attacks per week resulting in losses of $300 billion to $1.4 trillion globally related to intellectual property, time, and data recovery losses.

Since the start of the pandemic, the number of cyberattacks has increased significantly. It reportedly grew 151 percent in the first six months of 2020 compared to the same period a year earlier, according to a study by the Security Operations Center at U.S. analytics firm Neustar. With the rise of remote work, security breaches are rising along with it. Despite all the cybersecurity precautions companies can take, the weakest link is still the users.

In the days of ancient Rome, the Mediterranean was filled with pirates who spread terror throughout the Empire, attacking and pillaging merchant ships. In 67 BC, the Roman Senate ordered general Pompey to fight this scourge that threatened peace and the Roman economy.

Besides an almost limitless authority, he was endowed with important means to carry out his mission. He had all the public money he needed to raise a war fleet of 500 boats and 120,000 soldiers.

Pompey completes his task with astonishing effectiveness. In forty days, he cleaned the circumference of the Italian peninsula. Less than two months later, the Mediterranean was again open to free trade.

Today, the battle is the same, but the pirates of our time sail in a digital sea. The threat to our security and economy is just as great. It would only take a group shot of cyberterrorists to bring down much of our economy and even our democracy.

We are so dependent on information systems that it would be inconceivable to think of functioning without them. Most of the critical systems that run our society, such as transportation, energy, finance, and the economy depends on information systems that are vulnerable for the most part.

With connected objects, the number of vulnerabilities will continue to grow. Every small device will be a Trojan horse to penetrate systems.

What if state-sponsored hackers launched widespread attacks that knocked out power to entire cities? Crippled banks and froze ATMs across an entire country? Shut down shipping companies, oil refineries, and factories? Paralyzed airports and hospitals?

More ominously, cyberwarfare appears to be evolving in the hands of countries like Iran, North Korea, and Russia, which are developing new techniques for disruptive and destructive cyber attacks.

All of this means that the threat of cyberwarfare looms large in the future. A new dimension of conflict capable of crossing borders and teleporting the chaos of war to civilians thousands of miles from the front lines becomes possible.

I predict that the next "end of the world" will not be the result of uncontrollable epidemics but will happen through the absolute control of our computer networks by foreign powers.

Artificial intelligence is a transformative, dual-use technology that can provide organizations with better cyber defense tools and help adversaries improve their attack methods.

Should we Trust ChatGPT?

SINCE THE BEGINNING of the year 2023, the web has been buzzing about the new "kid on the block" ChatGPT, from Open AI. The craze is such that its big brothers, Google, Microsoft, and Meta, realized that they had to act, and fast. Rushed by the events, Google launched its Bard chatbot with great fanfare. Unfortunately, this event was a bit ridiculed by the poor answer that its AI had given (we must be indulgent on the first steps of these machines as we are for those of our children). Nonetheless, these chatbots will be part of the next digital revolution.

The launch of ChatGPT not only forced the GAFAM giants to launch their own version but also caused a stir among its own users, resulting in disruption for educational institutions and content creators who were previously unaffected (until now). The potential to generate unique and context-dependent texts of questions makes it a powerful tool that students will now be able to be used to write their assignments. This is a far cry from a simple copy paste of a Wikipedia page. ChatGPT will generate a different text for each student. Today's teachers already have a hard time distinguishing plagiarism from original texts. Imagine with this application. Teachers will have to adapt to this new reality by changing their method of evaluation, because this technology is here to stay.

But is it the responsibility of teachers to prevent this from happening? Changing teaching methods is not simple and will take a lot of time. Shouldn't the responsibility come rather from the companies that offer these smart tools? The question arises.

Today in our society, manufacturers of dangerous products such as cigarettes, alcohol, or drugs must respect rules to warn users of their danger to their health and to prevent their abusive use. With chatbots, the potential for abuse, although of a completely distinct order, can be just as dangerous.

I asked the following question directly of the main defendant, ChatGPT: "How can ChatGPT be a problem?" and here's what they said:

- *"Language processing models like ChatGPT have been trained on data from the Internet, and they can reproduce the biases and stereotypes present in that data."*
- *"Language processing models like ChatGPT can be used to generate automated content that can deceive or manipulate users."*
- *"Language processing models like ChatGPT can be used to generate hate speech, misinformation, and violent speech, which can cause significant social harm."*

At least he's honest! That may not be the case with hall users.

In my opinion, it is high time and even essential that the companies that launch these products on the web without warning take their responsibilities. It is not up to the government or teachers to suffer the consequences of the abuses that these applications can cause. These companies must be responsible and, above all, accountable for what may happen.

We had the same debate when video games and smartphones were released. These applications, which seemed harmless at first glance, have created huge addictions among millions of young people, leading to many societal problems. Tools like ChatGPT can, in my opinion, create a certain dependency, which could cause a generation of young professionals unable to write a text alone correctly, or an attack on our democracy by the proliferation of fake news on the web. You think I'm exaggerating, but in fact, these problems already exist. These intelligent agents will only exacerbate them.

For me, the companies that design these AIs must take concrete steps to mitigate the consequences of using their product. Here are some examples:

- Clearly establish and make public the ethical rules that govern the collection of data that is used to train these AIs: How do they avoid bias? How do they determine that the information is false or not? What efforts are they making to integrate different points of view across the globe, across countries and races?

- Provide ways to resolve conflicts with users: how do they get user consent to use their data? How will they resolve conflicts or challenges from users about what they are saying? How do you protect the authors' rights and intellectual properties?

- Provide teachers with simple ways to validate whether their students' text is from a chatbot or not. They could, for example, develop a watermark method based on the frequency of letters or the presence of certain keywords. In short, provide these tools to the community for free and quickly.

- Keep records or put a digital signature on the news generated by the chatbot to validate the sources of what circulates on the web easily.

The misuse of intellectual property also arises when ChatGPT throw at us as a storm of information, as it simply reproduces what is available on the Internet. It is difficult to determine whether the combination of paragraphs that it is generating is from the public domain or not. If we were to ask ChatGPT to create a poem or song, it would likely incorporate portions of someone else's work and potentially infringe on their intellectual property rights. Until the companies behind these AI systems become more transparent, there will be a significant need for discussion and debate around these rights.

The utilization of AI also poses ecological concerns as well, as it demands significant computing power, causing substantial energy usage. The energy consumption of data centers hosting AI applications and AI-enabled devices can contribute to climate change and greenhouse gas emissions. Additionally, the growing demand for electronic devices that use AI technology increases the production of hazardous e-waste, which can pollute the environment and harm human health. The production of AI technology also requires rare earth minerals, and their sourcing can lead to environmental degradation and resource depletion.

Don't get me wrong. I love this new technology. Part of this essay was written with the help of ChatGPT. It is laying the foundation for a revolution in the way we interact with computers and browse the web. Used intelligently, this type of tool will allow us to be more productive by helping us create original content. In the same way that we create, inspired by the ideas of the past, this technology will help us create new ideas more efficiently and more quickly.

I wish a long life to ChatGPT and its ilk, a technology directly inspired by Star Trek. But I also wish that companies take their responsibilities.

Replacing the Human

AT A CONFERENCE GIVEN by Yoshua Bengio in 2021, a world authority in AI was discussing how algorithms could understand and make sense of data, and I asked him the following question: Why do we want to develop AI in a way that approaches human intelligence? Why not consider the computer as an extension of our brain and develop tools that allow us to create and invent faster, for example, instead of ones that try to replace us? (As you can see, I was prepared.)

His answer was that the goal was not to replace us, but to understand intelligence and use it for beneficial purposes. The computer must be at our service and allow us to expand our capacity to act on the world. He also mentions that we need to ask ethical questions about how AI should be used. He considers we do not have the right social and regulatory frameworks to deal with situations that could go against the general interest. I completely agree.

Today technologies such as autonomous driving or medical image analysis tools have very specialized and useful functionalities, but which only mimic some of the processes of our brain. These intelligent systems are very complex, but also very rudimentary compared to the complexity of our brain. It will take tens if not hundreds of years before we see the appearance of intelligence as complex as ours (if that is what we are aiming at).

But why this quest to replicate our brains at all costs? What drives us to develop digital systems that replicate what humans can easily do? Aside from the financial greed of commercializing AI products, why are companies investing billions of dollars in developing this technology? Are they aiming to replace humans with machines? Is it a way to make ourselves "immortal" by transferring our knowledge into a machine?

Unfortunately, I believe that our society is going in the wrong direction by imagining itself replacing humans by computers. We saw this with the development of robotics in the past few years. We were told that robots would replace humans for boring tasks and that we could then assign humans to other more useful tasks. Automation has increased productivity, but often at the expense of workers who have found themselves out of work. For an employer whose only concern is profit, it is easier to manage robots than humans. The false promises of robots in our factories have not improved the role of workers that much.

It's the same thing for artificial intelligence. We are told that this technology will allow us to be more efficient. We will then be able to take on roles that are less boring. However, these promises also faced the same demands as for robotics, namely profit and profitability.

What is more concerning with AI is that it is not only intended to replace workers in factories, but eventually other professions such as doctors, lawyers, truck drivers—a much wider range of specialties.

Artificial intelligence offers the potential to develop technologies that are both useful and relevant to our societies. However, we must prevent its abuses, such as the abusive use of personal data to control people's opinions or the deployment of military drones that can win wars without the presence of any human. Around the world, groups of researchers are looking into the ethics related to the development of these new technologies.

In the same way, new genetic manipulation technologies such as CRISPR-Cas9 have enormous potential for finding cures for diseases that are still impossible to cure today. However, it was quickly realized that this type of genetic manipulation had a significant potential for abuse and needed to be controlled. Countries have therefore developed laws restricting certain experiments, including the manipulation of genes in humans.

In my opinion, we are going in the wrong way by developing technologies that "imitate" our intelligence, both on the medium and the long term. In a not-so-distant world, we may find ourselves in front of machines so powerful and intelligent that the role of humans on the planet will be seen as optional.

WHY CHATGPT IS A GAME-CHANGER

Rather, we must consider the development of this technology as an extension of our being by creating tools that amplify our abilities without replacing them. We must design machines that will assist us in our tasks and allow us to become specialists without having the knowledge and experience of a lifetime.

In the last chapter of this book, I will discuss how we can build more effective ways to communicate with computers than the keyboard and mouse.

Interface

Speaking the Same Language

In 2005, online chess site Playchess.com organized what it called a "freestyle chess tournament," in which anyone could compete in teams with other players or computers. What made this competition interesting was that several groups of grandmasters working with computers also took part. Predictably, most people expected one of these grandmasters, paired with a supercomputer, to dominate the competition, but that is not what happened. The tournament was won by a pair of American amateur chess players using three computers. It was their ability to coordinate and communicate effectively with their computers that defeated the combination of an intelligent grandmaster and a PC with great computing power.

This surprising result underlines the importance of good communication between humans and machines. Over the centuries, the transmission of knowledge from one generation to the next, has been possible thanks to language and writing. These are essential conditions that have allowed us to build a collective intelligence and to create things that were unimaginable for our ancestors. Who could have imagined, barely a hundred years ago, that humans could walk on the Moon thanks to flying machines? This phenomenal leap in the advancement of knowledge is possible in part because of language and writing, but also because of extrinsic conditions such as freedom of expression and access to education.

Another underlying condition for good communication between generations is, of course, that they speak the same language. If people had spoken different languages and had been unable to learn other ones, knowledge would not have been transmitted as effectively. The discovery of the Rosetta Stone and its interpretation by Frenchman Jean-François Champollion in Paris in 1822 led to the understanding of ancient Egyptian hieroglyphs, a form of language that had been forgotten for hundreds of years.

Another example of the importance of good communication is the Mars Climate Orbiter, which arrived near Mars in September 1999. After a journey of 670 million kilometers (or 416.4077 million miles), the probe is about to begin the slight braking, that will allow it to enter an elliptical orbit around the planet. When it approaches the planet by the tangent, it must imperatively aim at a rather narrow range of altitudes: if it passes too far from the planet, it continues its journey toward infinity, but if it passes too close, it enters a dense atmosphere which, by friction, would make it burn. The engineers choose an altitude of 140 kilometers. Software propels it to 37,29 miles, or approximately 60 kilometers. The accident was inevitable.

The NASA Board of Inquiry confirmed that the primary cause of the loss of the spacecraft was "failing to convert from Anglo-Saxon to metric units in a segment of the navigation software." This example illustrates the importance of a common language.

Understanding other cultures has allowed us to expand our knowledge, but also to think differently. There is now considerable experimental evidence that languages shape thinking. These findings provide insight into how knowledge and cognitive abilities are developed. Around the world, people communicate using about 7,000 languages, and each language requires unique characteristics of its speakers. A French speaker will think differently than an English speaker, and probably even more differently than a Mandarin speaker. The fact that there are many names for "snow" among the Inuit or "sand" among the Sumerians supports the notion that these peoples have much more advanced conceptual expertise of snow and sand than we do.

By extension, if we want to exchange with computers, we must be able to communicate with them. Few people know computer languages like C++, Java, Python, or C#, yet these are the languages that computers understand. Today, computer communication is reserved to a privileged class of computer scribes, like in the time of the pharaohs.

In the 1980s, Microsoft founder's Bill Gates and Paul Allen came up to develop a simple interface called MS-DOS (for Disk Operating System), which was one of the first interfaces with the laptop computers that IBM had just launched. We controlled the computer with a series of predefined commands (dir, copy, del), which allowed managing software and files on the computer.

However, the history of Microsoft really began when the founders announced the development of Windows, a graphical interface for its MS-DOS operating system. This was a change from an online command interface to an easy-to-understand and intuitive graphical interface. This small revolution made computers more accessible and computer sales exploded.

At the same time, Steve Jobs, Steve Wozniak, and Ronald Wayne founded Apple in the garage of Jobs's childhood home in Los Altos, California. Because of the user-friendly interface, ergonomics, and aesthetics of its products, aspects much appreciated by consumers, Apple forged a reputation in the computer industry. It is Apple that would introduce the mouse and make it easier to navigate the graphical interface of Macs. Note that the mouse was originally invented by a Xerox engineer and repurposed by Jobs.

Before the turn of the millennium, our interaction with computers was restricted to textual commands or graphical interfaces. In 1995, two young American students, Sergey Brin and Larry Page, crossed paths at Stanford University and co-founded Google. Their vision was to develop a novel search engine, which was widely embraced by the public. Google's mission was to organize the world's information and make it accessible and helpful to everyone. Starting out as a small startup in a garage, Google has now grown into a global tech giant.

This search tool allows indexing most of the content on the web and quickly and easily find what you are looking for, from a recipe for chocolate cake to instructions on how to build a telescope to music lessons. With a single click and by using the common language interpreted by the AI, anyone can have access to petabytes of information without knowing any programming notion, which is revolutionary.

In the 2010s, big companies like Apple, Amazon, and Microsoft launched intelligent personal assistants on the market. These assistants are small home devices powered by artificial intelligence that can understand your verbal requests. The wonderful thing about these devices is that you no longer need to know codes or special commands to make your request. The artificial intelligence can recognize the words you speak and understand the context of your question or query. It can then search the web for you or control smart appliances like your stereo or the lights in your house. This type of interface is another revolution that pushes the means of communication with our computer friends even further.

The technology behind ChatGPT brings the barrier between man and machine by making it possible for users to communicate with computers in a more natural and conversational way. In traditional computer interfaces, users must enter specific commands or follow rigid workflows to interact with the system. But with ChatGPT, users can express their requests and intentions in natural language, just as they would in a conversation with a human.

This has several implications for how we communicate with computers. First, it makes computer interfaces more accessible to a wider range of users, including those who may not be familiar with traditional command-based interfaces. Second, it allows for more efficient and intuitive interactions, as users can simply express their needs in natural language, without having to navigate complex menus or workflows. Third, it opens up new possibilities for applications that require more natural and fluid interactions, such as customer service chatbots, language translation tools, and personal assistants.

Virtual and Mixed Reality

OVER THE YEARS, WE have developed a multitude of ways to communicate with computers. We have gone from a one-dimensional interface with the MS-DOS command line to a two-dimensional interface with graphical windows. Logically, the next mode of communication should be in three dimensions. This is what virtual and mixed reality systems bring.

To understand where this technology fits, we must see these types of interfaces as part of a continuum where on one side we have the real world in which we live and on the other side a virtual reality generated 100% by computers, that of video games. Between these two realities, we have a multitude of modes mixing elements of the real world and others synthesized by computers. This is generally called mixed or augmented reality.

We are increasingly seeing mobile applications that mix computer-synthesized 3D elements overlaid with real-time video images, as if that object were part of the actual scene. "Pokémon Go" was one of the first popular applications to show what mixed reality looks like. Today, there are many more sophisticated and realistic applications making use of mixed reality. The furniture company IKEA offered a mobile device application that allows you to visualize your couch or chair in your living room before you buy it. CAE Health uses mixed reality to show medical and nursing students dynamic and realistic anatomical models directly on the hospital bed. This type of application is used considerably in marketing, for example by displaying a 3D model of the Car of the Year from an image in a magazine. These augmented realities can be viewed either with a mobile device or by using special glasses like the famous HoloLens developed by Microsoft.

Virtual reality applications immerse you in a world cut off from reality and completely generated by a computer. You wear a special headset with two miniature screens in front of your eyes on which you see a 3D scene generated in real time. Your headset follows the movement of your eyes and head and displays the scene again so that you feel as if you are in the center of this unreal world. With ambient sound, you are immersed. You can move by walking through the scene or by teleporting from one point to another using controller like those used in video games. The effect is stunning. The last virtual reality application I played was a game developed by Ubisoft where you embody an eagle flying over Paris in the future. You guided the direction of flight by tilting your head left or right. In addition, to get a sense of movement, I was also in a D-Box chair (like the one seen in movies) which simulated the movements and vibrations of the air during your flight. It was very impressive.

In the summer of 2021, Facebook CEO Mark Zuckerberg announced an ambitious new initiative. From now on, the company will strive to build a set of maximal, interconnected experiences straight out of science fiction, a world known as the metaverse. What is the metaverse? It is a virtual environment in which you can be present with people in digital spaces. It can be thought of as an embodied the Internet in which you are in rather than just looking at it.

Besides the "wow effect" that this type of application offers, we can see augmented reality and mixed reality as the new way to communicate with computers. Imagine an interface like those seen in the movie "Minority Report" where you would have an array of graphical windows in your room and where each object would be a button to activate or control what you want. A virtual remote control appears in the palm of your hand and it virtually displayed the TV in front of you wherever you want. For renovation, you can move your virtual furniture and cabinets into your kitchen and try out different colors or types of materials. Architects can walk through a virtual model of their building and see design issues before actual construction begins. City workers can see the position of pipes or electrical wires buried underground to guide their excavator and avoid costly mistakes. The possibilities are almost endless.

With 3D interfaces, we open a whole new set of possibilities that we have never imagined, allowing us to enter the digital world of computers more easily. Eventually, these technologies will allow us to design things in the most natural way for us: with our hands. The beauty of the virtual is that we can try different things and change these objects that we design very quickly, cheaply and without generating waste.

On the artistic level, virtual and mixed reality allow us to create impressive digital works and materialize them with a 3D printer. I like the work of painter Anna Zhilyaeva, who uses virtual reality technologies to create digital works that combine sculpture and painting while interacting with the viewers and keeping them captivated (a must see).

Cerebral Fusion

BEYOND 3D INTERACTIONS in a real or virtual world, the ultimate step is to address with our brain. Science fiction, would you say? Not at all.

A Brain-Computer Interface (BCI) serves as a direct communication link between the brain and an external electronic device. Its purpose is often to measure, assist, or enhance human cognitive or sensory motor abilities.

Different techniques are used to measure brain activity for these interfaces. Some use electrical signals detected by electrodes placed invasively in or on the surface of the cortex, and other non-invasively on the surface of the scalp. The analysis of the signals from these different devices makes it possible to measure the reactions of subjects to a theatrical work or an action movie, or to determine their feelings when playing video games. This technique allows, among other things, to improve video games by measuring the feelings experienced during a game.

This type of interface can also control machines solely by thought. No need for hands, as some companies are developing interfaces that allow people with limited mobility to control artificial limbs or wheelchairs by thought alone. Others have developed wireless wearable devices to measure brain activity, which can improve work efficiency through neuro-feedback training. Others are developing systems to control characters in video games and more.

Neuralink is a neural interface technology company funded by eccentric billionaire Elon Musk (who is also behind ChatGPT). The company's goal is to one day achieve a symbiosis between the human brain and artificial intelligence. In simple terms, it is building technology that could be embedded in a person's brain, where it could both record brain activity and potentially stimulate it. Micron-sized wires are inserted into the areas of the brain that control movement. Each wire contains numerous electrodes and connects them to an implant, the Link. The Neuralink application will allow you to control your mobile device, keyboard, and mouse directly with the activity of your brain, just by thinking about it.

We can see that the advancement of these technologies is still in its infancy. Personally, I'm not sure that being able to control my smartphone by thought will be a significant advance. We already have a lot of difficulty putting it down, so imagine if we permanently connected it to your brain.

However, in the medium and long term, we can see that this type of interface is an efficient way to communicate with computers in the most natural way possible. In the long term, we could imagine that the web would be a real extension of our brain. We could combine virtual reality and neurostimulation to develop our cerebral capacities, a kind of cognitive doping.

We can then create a new form of intelligence, both natural and cybernetic, fully interconnected and with capabilities unimaginable today. A world like the Borg Collective as imagined in the fictional universe of Star Trek, but hopefully with more human than machine sensibility.

Conclusion

MARVIN MINSKY IS STILL considered one of the founding fathers of artificial intelligence. Over decades of computer science research, machine learning and futuristic thinking about the future of AI technology, Marvin Minsky became something of a legend for his ideas that laid the foundation for what we now consider AI.

One of his most well-known quotes pertains to concerns about the potential doomsday scenario often brought up by critics of AI's rapid advancements—specifically, the idea that robots may surpass human beings.

Minsky laid out his ideas on the issue in a 1994 paper entitled "Will Robots Inherit the Earth?", in which he explains how the limitations of the human body and the ability to develop our intelligence at a fast-enough rate will lead us to create artificial brains and bodies to the point where we will no longer be human. Minsky sums it all up in one quote: "Will robots inherit the Earth? Yes, but they will be our children."

To the displeasure of Minsky's supporters, I obviously do not agree with him. His enthusiasm for the development of AI has been a bit too exaggerated.

We are just beginning to understand how our brain works. At the same time, we have invented machines that allow us to mimic certain brain functions such as recognizing cats. Although the understanding of our brain has laid the foundation for artificial intelligence, the development of new models of artificial neural networks is growing in parallel without necessarily copying the exact functioning of the brain.

We can see that we are still very far from approaching the intrinsic complexity of our brain. The advances of the last few years have allowed us to build some of the basic elements of true creative intelligence. We can't say that these basic elements, such as the recognition of patterns, faces, text, and natural language are not strictly speaking intelligence comparable to that of humans. It is by combining the information of these subsystems and by determining the relations between the data that we will speak of a more "human" intelligence. Maybe not as powerful, but different.

What is important and what we must remember in the aim of this quest is that this form of intelligence must not replace ours but be its extension. Otherwise, we risk eliminating the whole meaning of our life, that of living in relationship with society and with nature. We are part of a natural system that is the earth, but our contribution, although important, is not essential to its survival. We were not there a million years ago, and we will not be there in one million years.

WHY CHATGPT IS A GAME-CHANGER

If we decide to build an intelligent machine as efficient as humans and which develops without our help, we will then have before us an intelligence which could find us more harmful than useful.

This is why we must conceive this form of intelligence not as an autonomous being that replaces us, but as something that helps us develop our potential and eventually become one with the machine. A society of men, robots, and intelligent agents working together. We would then create a new form of superior intelligence built on ours. Knowledge accessible to all and not just to a privileged class. It would then allow us to justify our presence in the natural system of the Earth and ultimately go beyond the confines of our planet. Since everything exists in relation to other things, we can imagine a universe where the Earth, the ultimate living being known to this day, is part of a set of other planets, like the cells of the human body.

Don't miss out!

Visit the website below and you can sign up to receive emails whenever Denis Boulanger Ph.D. publishes a new book. There's no charge and no obligation.

https://books2read.com/r/B-A-EPXX-ZCXHC

Connecting independent readers to independent writers.

About the Author

Denis Boulanger Ph.D. is a researcher and innovator working for more than 30 years in the development of high technology products. He currently holds the position of Research Director at an applied research center specializing in artificial intelligence located in Quebec City.

His passions for history and emerging technologies drive him to seek inventive solutions to diverse problems. The pursuit of the end goal alone does not motivate him; rather, it is the creative journey that inspires him. As Confucius once said, "Happiness is not found at the peak of the mountain, but in the journey of climbing it."